Fixing Leadership

Advance Praise for Fixing Leadership

"In a world where leadership roles are often assumed without any training and new managers are left alone to figure out how to create work cultures, cultivate careers, delegate, and get results from their teams, this book emerges as a beacon of insight and wisdom. Fixing Leadership is a transformative guide that delves into the very essence of modern leadership. Stan's authentic and compelling writing offers practical advice, solid research, and a comprehensive look at being a great leader, no matter the industry. Whether you're stepping into a leadership role for the first time or a seasoned manager looking to take their leadership to the next level, Fixing Leadership is a must-read."

- Dr. Marshall Goldsmith, the Thinkers50 #1 Executive Coach and New York Times bestselling author of *The Earned Life*, *Triggers*, and *What Got You Here Won't Get You There.*

"The most important leadership quality today is vulnerability. To share a connection with others we need to be vulnerable ourselves. Stan's story is one of vulnerability and a passion for developing and leading others. If you are a leader, or want to be one, Stan gives us insight as to how we can fix leadership today."

- Rod Miller, Past President CPHR Alberta

"In his new book, Fixing Leadership, Stan Peake does a masterful job of showing us what's missing in leadership, giving us a new way to think about it, and inspiring us to take action. He also talks about how things have changed and what exactly has changed, so leaders and organizations can be more successful today. Stan's comprehensive research, combined with his rich reservoir of life and leadership experience, positions him as a preeminent teacher. Thank you, Stan, for empowering both seasoned and aspiring leaders to make a lasting impact on the world!"

- Robb Holman, Global Gurus top 30 leadership speaker and author of *Lead the Way, All In, Move the Needle*, and *Lessons from Abdul*

"In his most recent book, "Fixing Leadership", Stan Peake identifies the most common leadership skill gaps from the lens of leaders and executive coaches, then through interviews with successful leaders, he distills their advice on how to address these pervasive leadership gaps. "Fixing Leadership" offers insightful reflections on what makes a great leader. You will come away with practical and intentional approaches to become a better leader. Stan Peake adds value again!"

- Patricia van de Sande, CA, CPA, ICD.D, GCB.D, CEO - Bridge Advisory Group

"Fixing Leadership is an excellent read. Everyone from the C-Suite, Founders, Direct Reports, HR/HCM, and colleagues should have a copy of "Fixing Leadership"! Some may be reminders and a lot will have a fresher view in regards to leaving "leadership better than you found it"!

- Michael Palmer, **Vice President, Operations, Innosol Health**

"Fixing Leadership is a shining landmark of wisdom. With an unmistakably genuine and engaging voice, Peake offers a potent blend of actionable advice, real-life research and a profound exploration of what truly defines exceptional leadership. Peake not only sheds light on the leadership gaps that plague many organizations, but also offers profound reflections on the essence of what makes leadership truly impactful. Through meticulous research and insightful interviews with leadership luminaries, he takes readers on a growth path, dissecting key concepts before culminating in a powerful 'call to action'. Each chapter unfolds like a map, illuminating the complex challenges and powerful opportunities that define leadership in today's world."

- Matteo Borgna, the youngest Harvard Business School Online chapter organizer in history

"Any leader who wants to prioritize and focus their development for the most effective impact would be wise to read Fixing Leadership. Although the book highlights leadership is not "broken" we need to fix how we teach, learn and live leadership. There are many validating data points to help guide any open-minded leader who wants to shift their capability to achieve greater results through a lasting coaching approach."

- Brian Hughes, named by CEOWeekly as one of the Top 15 Leadership Coaches of 2024

Dedication

A wise man once told me that you are either a 'producer' or 'consumer' in life. This book is written for all the producers out there who give more than they take. The world needs better leaders, and it starts with those who lead by embracing this simple, yet powerful philosophy: try to leave your corner of the world a little bit better than you found it.

Fixing Leadership

Introduction 11

One: Leadership was the only path 13

Two: We've lost our path 17

Three: The numbers don't lie 25

Four: Beacons of hope 41

Five: One size fits one leadership 75

Six: The DNA of tomorrow's leader 143

Seven: Call to action 149

Appendix 151

Acknowledgements 171

Introduction

Leadership is one big paradox.

While you may question the effectiveness of *that* former boss, would you ever question whether or not leadership itself is important? The overwhelming majority of us would say no. This means we generally accept leadership as an essential part of building any team or organization. Tell you something you didn't know, right? Here's the paradox. Leadership is almost universally accepted as essential, yet we have no universally accepted definition for leadership. We know we need it, but we don't know *exactly* what it is.

Trying to include all of the requisite traits of great leaders into a singular definition is like trying to capture lightning in a bottle. Everyone knows great leadership when they see it, but can anyone define it?

This book, unfortunately, won't solve that problem. This book is intended to identify, understand, and help solve the much bigger problem that stems from that first problem. The real problem is, if we can't define leadership, how on Earth would we effectively teach it? And if we don't know how to teach leadership effectively and consistently, then we don't know how to build better leaders, or better prepare leaders for the what the job entails.

I've been coaching in one form or another since 1992. At the time of publication, that's 32 years of learning my craft. In that time, I've had the privilege of speaking at more conferences that I can remember. It's been my life's work to lift others to their potential, and through coaching, speaking, and writing, I've been able to do that for hundreds of thousands of leaders. This is the sample size of data through which I've come to understand the problem.

The problem is not that leadership is broken. The problem is that we simply have nowhere near the number of capable leaders ready for what challenges lie before them. We have (collectively) done a poor job of preparing would-be leaders for the ever-evolving role that is leadership. We teach the same concepts that (maybe) worked in the past to leaders who face completely new and more complex challenges than ever before.

My goal through this book, and through the years I have left to serve others, is to help solve this problem. We need more, better leaders now than we ever have before. The state of leadership readiness has never been more dire, at a time when great leadership has never been more needed.

Let's understand this problem better together so that we can build solutions that serve us all.

1

Leadership was the only path

Let's start things off with a little bit of irony. I am trying to reinvent how we prepare would-be leaders for leadership roles, and I was fired from my first management job. While it may be perfectly logical to call into question my credibility for such an ambitious goal, I believe most of you will come to a different conclusion. My unique journey into leadership has allowed me a vantage point into a flawed system that is failing millions of leaders and organizations worldwide. It is perhaps exactly because I was an outlier that I was able to gain the perspective most leaders and organizations seem to have missed.

We don't know how to predictably, consistently produce capable leaders, and that's a huge problem at a time when we've never needed more great leaders.

I used to think my path was unconventional; one of the original mavericks. I 'fell into' leadership, as opposed to ending up there after attending the best schools and demonstrating the merit and valor we attribute to the great leaders of history. I had maybe three years' experience as a personal trainer (the average career length of a trainer at the time), and the person before me quit. It was pretty much a case of "you'll do until we find someone better."

I had always assumed before you took a management or leadership job of any kind, you would receive some sort of formal training. Management 101. How to be a great boss. What to do when your employees come to you with big challenges. Nope. Nada. Zilch. By the way, I take full responsibility for being let go from that role. It was one of the best things that could have happened to me, because looking back, I never would have thrived there.

Nearly 25 years, and seven leadership roles later, I've seen a similar pattern. Most of the best leaders I've worked with or coached 'fell into' leadership too. Even entrepreneurs who start their own companies often don't imagine leading a team. Even if they do, it's not why they started the company.

I've started a few of my own companies, and I've worked for some of the world's most recognizable brands. Some trends I've picked up over the last quarter century in terms of what I've been taught;

- Opening and closing procedures
- Above average sales training from just one of the five companies I worked for in a sales capacity
- How to answer the phone
- How to fill out an expense report
- How to greet customers
- How to maintain fitness equipment to extend its' life cycle another two – five years during my time in the fitness industry

This list is not shared to insult or belittle any employer, I was fortunate to work for and with every company that I did. The point is that there was no formal leadership training, even with two global organizations I worked for. I hired at least 100 people before I had a business partner share interview questions and techniques they'd learned from a book. That's right, I made hiring and firing decisions over 100 times before receiving any formal training besides 'here's the sheet with the interview questions we ask'.

This is not to say that great leadership, recruitment, interviewing, onboarding and training programs don't exist in the corporate world. It's simply my experience that I had to learn those skills from mentors, other entrepreneurs, or on my own dime through courses, books, and making costly mistakes.

At this point, you might be wondering how, or why, I've chosen coaching leaders as a career. Why stick with a profession you were fired from, and then not trained for? Like many of you, I was bit by the passion bug.

Let me take you back a few years. I was bullied as a youngster, and after picking up my dad's weights, I turned to football. I found acceptance, community, and two other things that would change my life by playing football; passion and mentorship.

I loved playing football, and from the age of 14 to 19 I had a reason to stay out of trouble. I was part of something bigger than myself, so the concept of consequences resonated with me at an age that doesn't for so many others. Just ask anyone who's raised teenagers! Instead of hanging out at convenience stores smoking and shoplifting, I was either at practice or lifting weights. I stayed out of trouble at an age when so many young adults can't possibly understand the long-range consequences of their mistakes.

In the form of mentorship, my high school football coach Joe Stambene saw something in me before I saw it in myself. He pulled me into his office after the first semester of grade 10, and asked me to explain every time I was late, and every absence on my report card. Let's just say there was much less truancy the next semester!

Stambene's approach built a powerhouse. We lost just three games in three years, and we won a city championship, but it's the way he did it that was special. My coach built a winning team through character, not just talent. Not surprisingly, he would go on to win four more city championships and a provincial football title in his career.

Those experiences- finding a passion for something bigger than yourself, and having someone care enough about you to truly invest in you – they change you. At least, they changed me. You'd have to ask my team if I'm a good leader or not, but I'm sure you now understand why leadership became a passion; a calling for me.

Of course, there were many other experiences along the way. I worked for a boss under criminal investigation right before I worked for someone who was named one of Canada's 'Top 40 Under 40'; named so for raising more than $6M for charity in a business that might have been doing $6M in revenue at the time.

I had a boss who challenged me to go back to school to make sure my career options weren't limited. He didn't just care about me making money for the company, he cared about my future.

> *Unless I was going to be a narcissistic leach who took from others and never gave, my experiences set me on a course that leadership was my only path.*

After my family, and so many others gave so much, I'd be a leader if I was a janitor, computer scientist, or painter. Unfortunately, not everyone can be so fortunate. Not everyone finds a great mentor early. Millions rely on 'the system' to prepare them, only to find out that in most cases – it won't.

2

We've lost our path

If you read the introduction, you read that I've been coaching (athletes and executives) for 32 years. Most coaches tend to think in 'abundance mindset'; there is enough for us all. Unfortunately, many decision-makers in business operate from a place of 'scarcity mindset' thinking they *'must make due with our share of finite resources'*.

Greed and scarcity have a lot to do with how businesses are run. Unfortunately, they have for a very long time. Research into basic human psychology tells us that our primary drivers are to seek out pleasure, and avoid pain. The problem is, from our purchase decisions to our business decisions, we tend to avoid pain 70% of the time, only seeking out pleasure 30% of the time[1]. In the grand scheme, we are risk averse, and we ask 'what if?' from a place of what could go wrong, not what could go right.

I've seen this play out far too many times;

- "Why would I spend all of this time and money training my team? They're just going to leave to become my competition"
- "Your department is a loss leader, that's why we don't have enough to spend on sales and marketing" (actual comment a client received from one of their peers on the leadership team. Our client was the head of safety and quality assurance)
- "We just don't have the money"
- "We're too busy with (literally anything). Let's look at implementing a (leadership or staff) training program in Q4"

I believe most of the people who say these things and think this way are good people. They are doing the best they can, making the best decisions they can with the time and information they are given. That's actually the problem. This is not a case of good versus evil. It's good versus *time*.

Even leaders with great capability have low capacity. "Do more with less" has made its way into the fabric of every organization on the planet with toxic results. Most leaders that I've spoken to believe a leader should have no more than 10 direct reports. Many feel more than six direct reports compromises their ability to do the job with sustainable results. This makes me feel much better about when I imploded in my second business having more than 50 direct reports.

Whether due to time pressure, the pace of change, or stiffening competition, in most cases, leaders must make timely decisions with an incomplete set of facts. They are juggling budgets, emotions, strong opinions, and consequences no matter which way they turn.

In many cases, business decisions come down to the best bad choice. It's not right or wrong, moral or immoral. It's "what choice won't get me fired?" or "what consequences can I live with?"

Profit and greed are at play however, and many people figuratively sell their souls for fame, money, or power. It's hard to do the right thing all the time, right? It's exhausting, 'why can't I catch a break?' you might ask yourself. 'Everyone else is cutting corners (or cheating the system), why shouldn't I?'

We tend to over-simplify the problem. It's not just good versus evil. It's not just good versus time. It's good versus time mixed with incomplete data mixed with high emotion mixed with a lack of formal training while also battling good versus evil.

Dr. Marilyn Taylor, Professor of Leadership Studies at Royal Roads University in Victoria, BC put it best.

> "Leadership can't just be taught as a set of skills and knowledge. This antiquated approach tends to set high potentials and future leaders up for failure. They may feel like they aren't effective in, or even ready, for leadership positions because they aren't experts, whereas true leaders need to navigate areas wherein they aren't experts, perhaps not even skilled. True leaders must lead through uncertainty, not just grab the helm when they are the most qualified and experienced in a given arena".

According to Taylor, "you can't teach leadership without being in it. In other words, one can't just read about leadership online and hope to be effective in the real world. Those in leadership must link any important lesson to action immediately, because talking about things without doing anything is not a useful pattern. Learning in this way doesn't influence behavior or move the needle".

From Dr. Taylor, I've come to understand that we try to teach leadership as a set of theories and academic principles. This fails in the real world because leaders are needed most during times of chaos, change, crisis, and uncertainty. Put simply, we try to teach people to know what to do, when the job is often 'what to do *when you don't know what to do'*.

Imagine you had to teach an entire high school how to drive. Would you sit them in a classroom for a week covering the theory of driving, then hand them the keys and say good luck? Of course not, that would be a catastrophe; however, that's exactly how we have been teaching leadership.

There's also a problem with the leadership development that we do offer. It hasn't changed much. In the next chapter, we'll be diving into some research on the state of leadership readiness. I was presenting some of this research with a group of energy industry leaders in Calgary, Alberta in 2022. In short, I was presenting what skills leaders didn't feel adequately prepared for. Basically, what the job required, but the training didn't properly cover.

One of those leaders, in typical Canadian fashion, apologized for challenging the research. "I'm sorry, but if you showed this research in 2000, or even 1980, wouldn't the answers be the same?"

This question made me consider the problem in yet another context. I'd already concluded that if we have skills gaps that business leaders are reporting, then we aren't doing enough to prepare them for the role of leadership. Based on this leaders' comment, if those gaps aren't changing over time, then we have a second problem. Most of the time what we are teaching isn't working. We either don't know what to teach, how to teach it, or worse – both. It's a downright scary equation.

Not enough training X ineffective training = poor leadership development

---

Of course, there are exceptions, but on the whole, corporate and private training solutions are failing. We are failing despite $366 billion spent globally each year (2019 statistics) on leadership development programs, which is expected to grow by another $15.78 billion from 2020 to 2025[2,3].

We are failing based on the above equation, but there's another problem.

Senior business leaders are retiring in droves. In fact, 10,000 Baby Boomers are retiring every day according to 2015 research[4]. This in large part explains why 84% of organizations surveyed anticipate a leadership shortfall within the next five years[4]. That last statistic becomes all the more sobering when you consider it, too, was based on 2015 research. By 2020, 77% of organizations surveyed had already experienced a leadership gap[5]. According to the same research, 71% of companies believe that there is a leadership capability gap among current leaders they feel are essential for future progress[5]. Furthermore, only 11% of human resource leaders surveyed feel they have a 'solid bench' to fill upcoming leadership role vacancies[5].

All of this research points to one irrefutable conclusion. We are losing leaders faster than we can replace them. With all other forces being held constant, if we cannot find existing or train new leaders to replace the vacancies being created, we will experience a worsening 'leadership vacuum'. The research is clear on the retention of existing leaders, and the ability to find new ones. So what does the research say on how we are preparing potential leaders for success in their roles?

In short, the research on the present state isn't much more promising. A shocking 59% of 500 managers surveyed who oversee one or two direct reports received no management training whatsoever prior to assuming their role[6]. The same is true for 41% of managers overseeing three to five direct reports[6].

The same study found that 42% of managers surveyed developed their leadership style simply by observing others[6].

Pulling all of these trends together, we have a massive and widening leadership gap. We have a gap in the number of leaders needed, the number of leaders available, and how we are fixing that gap through adequate, available leadership training. It's no mystery that we are short of great leaders to lead our organizations where they need to go. It's no mystery either that how we are developing new leaders isn't working well enough. So the multi-billion dollar question remains; how do we solve the problem?

It was this question exactly that led to studying the problem, rather than answering too quickly. In speaking with my colleagues in the world of leadership development, we had our ideas, but we wanted to understand the problem more holistically. We reached out to our network for help.

First, we reached out to 209 leaders in 29 countries to understand their experiences entering leadership. We asked, *"What leadership skills do you feel you weren't properly trained for when you started leading people?"*

We received 135 unique responses, which we then grouped into 13 macro trends.

Next, we reached out to our extensive network of executive coaches around the world. Because today's leaders are (implicitly or explicitly) expected to be coaches for their teams, at least part of the time, we wanted to hear from professional coaches, *"What coaching skills do you feel leaders (regardless of organization) need to learn to help lead their team(s) in today's world?"*

Our coaches came through with 61 unique responses, which we then compared against the same 13 macro trends from our leaders' survey. Finally, we combined responses, to see what skills our sample size of 315 professional leaders and coaches feel are most important to be teaching in leadership development and leadership onboarding programs.

Our next chapter breaks down the results from our leaders, our coaches, and the aggregate results, including demographic data.

3

The numbers don't lie

When my team and I wanted to understand the problem, we wanted to start in the trenches. We wanted to hear from leaders living the problem every day. We wanted to hear from leaders in business, not-for-profits, charities, the military, and even sporting and religious organizations. We wanted to understand what leadership skills they weren't being adequately prepared for as they assumed their roles.

We asked leaders, from those managing their first team, to a few with 45 years of leadership experience, "What leadership skills do you feel you weren't properly trained for when you started leading people?" We felt we needed to hear from those most affected by leadership development training – those the training was designed for!

There was one more reason we wanted to survey our network of leaders. Think back to when you started with your current company (or when you last had a boss for you entrepreneurs). Who did you go to in order to learn the administrative aspects of your new job? Who did you ask about what opportunities there were before you, or what a career road map might look like for you? And who did you turn to for coaching when your new job presented inevitable challenges or setbacks? Chances are the answer to all of these questions was your direct supervisor.

We've already established that leaders aren't getting enough leadership training to meet the demands of their jobs. So how much training do you think leaders are getting on how to be a competent coach for their teams? In the overwhelming majority of cases, that number is zero, yet the reality of their team remains the same – their boss is either the catalyst or the bottleneck to their growth. For these reasons we must teach leaders in business at least basic coaching skills!

We also wanted to hear from our extensive network of leadership and executive coaches. After all, they work with leaders at all levels every day to help them overcome their challenges and become better leaders!

In order to survey our network of coaches around the world, we conducted interviews, we sent surveys, we asked our teams, we even incorporated our research into some of our keynote addresses at conferences all over the world. We asked coaches, from three years of experience to more than 30 "what coaching skills should we be teaching leaders in business?"

Starting with our leaders, this is what our research uncovered.

Leaders surveyed: 209

Average years of leadership experience: 15.62

Figure 3.1: Leaders' experience

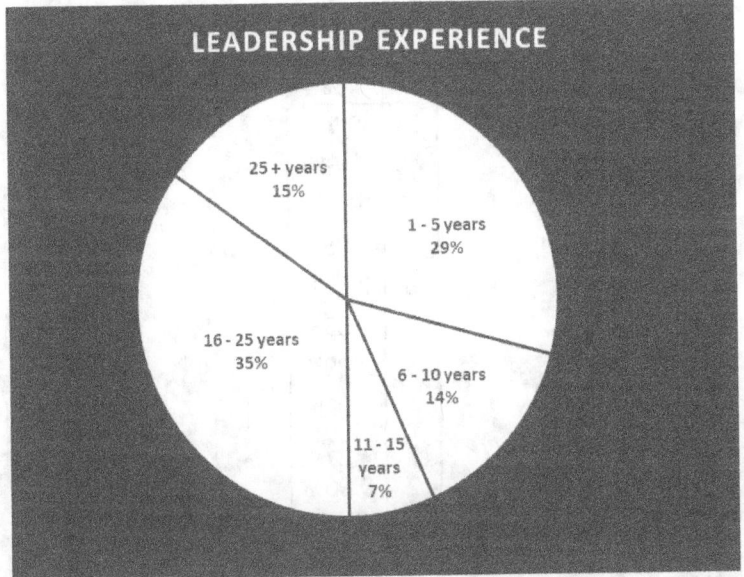

Demographics

Table 3.1: Leaders' geographical distribution by country

	Country	#	%
1	Canada	83	39.71%
2	United States	45	21.53%
3	UK	21	10.05%
4	Czech Republic	7	3.35%
5	China	6	2.87%
6	Ireland	5	2.39%
7	Italy	5	2.39%
8	Germany	4	1.91%
9	Belgium	3	1.44%
10	France	2	0.96%
11	Greece	2	0.96%
12	India	2	0.96%
13	Malta	2	0.96%
14	The Netherlands	2	0.96%
15	Poland	2	0.96%
16	Portugal	2	0.96%
17	Scotland	2	0.96%
18	Australia	1	0.48%
19	Bangladesh	1	0.48%
20	Brazil	1	0.48%
21	Brussels	1	0.48%
22	Central Europe	1	0.48%
23	Cyprus	1	0.48%
24	Latin America	1	0.48%
25	Nigeria	1	0.48%
26	Sweden	1	0.48%
27	Switzerland	1	0.48%
28	Turkey	1	0.48%
29	UAE	1	0.48%

Table 3.2: Leader's geographical distribution by continent

Continent	#
North America	128
Europe	64
Asia	8
Africa	4
South America	2
Australia	1

Leadership skill gaps

Through our analysis of the state of leadership training survey, we were able to group the 209 responses into 135 trends. The grouped raw responses of the top 10 trends are shown in Table 3.3 below.

Table 3.3: Skill gap raw responses

	What weren't you prepared/ trained for?	#	%
1	Managing/ resolving conflict	28	13.40%
2	Emotional intelligence	16	7.66%
T3	Giving feedback	15	7.18%
T3	Empathy	15	7.18%
5	How to lead each person (ie 1 size fits 1)	14	6.70%
6	Proper communication	13	6.22%
T7	No understanding/ training of what leadership is. Just given the title	12	5.74%
T7	How to be strategic/ lead with strategy/ systems	12	5.74%
T9	How to have difficult conversations	10	4.78%
T9	Holding others accountable	10	4.78%

Summary of findings

Only nine of 135 response trends we received were 'technical/ tactical' in nature. In other words, of 135 response trends, 126 required personal (self) and/ or inter-personal (other) leadership. Only skills like 'putting together a budget', 'privacy and security issues', and 'how to lead with strategy/ systems' were listed in our survey as skill gaps our leaders weren't necessarily prepared for. 'How hard fundraising is' was one of those skills, and one could argue this involves leading a team to raise funds, and dealing with donors, so there is a case to be made that 127 of our 135 skill gap trends (94.03%) are people-based soft skills, not 'technical/ tactical' knowledge-based skills.

When viewed through a macro-analysis and grouped together in terms of macro skills, our skills gaps paint a clearer picture of what leaders are telling us they are not getting enough of in terms of education, training, or experience. Table 3.4 demonstrates the macro trends found through our survey.

Table 3.4 Skill gap trends

Leaders' learning gaps	
"One size fits one leadership"	135
Communication	73
Giving and receiving feedback	73
Being supportive	70
Emotional intelligence	67
Managing conflict	65
Creating alignment	56
Leading self	51
Leading through culture	46
Strategic/ tactical	45
Holding others accountable	40
Diversity, Equity, Inclusion	18
Confidence building	12

It is important to remember that this is not an assessment of the priority of skills that leaders place in some sort of hierarchy. This is an amalgamation of the greatest gaps faced by the 207 leaders in our survey. For the purposes of understanding, here is how we defined each of the above macro skills.

1. "One size fits one leadership": the ability to customize directives, support, accountability, management and coaching to the unique values, motives, communicative style, and career stage for each team member.
2. Giving and receiving feedback:
    - the ability to avoid judgement, rationalization, excuses, or become emotionally triggered while receiving feedback.
    - The ability to deliver feedback from a place of support and best intentions, avoiding

judgement, or becoming emotionally reactive when delivering feedback.
3. Communication: the skills of active listening, as well as effective oral and written communication. This includes body language, paralanguage, and timing and mode of delivery. Each of these will be explained further in chapter five.
4. Being supportive: acting in the best interests of those you support, and being there for them through challenging situations, even as you may be the one challenging them.
5. Managing conflict: the ability to deflate emotionally charged situations, and to resolve inter-personal conflict among different stakeholders, within or even external to one's organization.
6. Emotional intelligence: the layered skill of;
    - Being self-aware enough to manage one's emotions, and know when you are feeling triggered or in conflict (and how to manage or improve your emotional state).
    - Being present enough to detect the emotional state of other stakeholders in any given situation.
    - Understanding contextual and situational elements relative to all parties.
    - Being able to choose appropriate actions, strategies, or communication keeping all the above moving parts in mind.
7. Leading self: asking oneself "how did I contribute to this challenge (or conflict)?" or "what's here for me to own?" when given feedback. It's often said that leaders look in the mirror first, and this is exactly what we mean. Leaders tend to their own garden before pointing out their neighbors' weeds.

8. Creating alignment: the ability to find potential intersection points between different, sometimes even competing, points of view. By 'creating alignment' we also refer to the ability to align motives among multiple stakeholders, as well as align personal and organizational lenses. Leaders know that what's good for the team is good for the business, and vice versa.
9. Strategic/ tactical: the more traditional business concepts like strategies, schedules, manufacturing, sales, and more. Leaders often refer to the strategic or tactical side of business as the 'X and O' aspects of running a business; whereas many leadership intangibles often get clumped together as 'soft skills'.
10. Leading through culture: means, to us, igniting the tactical aspects of strategy through the lens of why the strategy matters. Reinforcing that X, Y, or Z is the chosen strategy, because it helps fulfil the organizational purpose, bring us closer to our vision, and is an expression of living our values at the highest level.
11. Holding others accountable: is less about 'getting people in trouble' when they make a mistake, and more about holding high performers to their word. To be an accountable leader is to hold your team up to their potential, through systems like project management, through schedules, and most of all – through care.
12. Diversity, Equity, Inclusion: to avoid groupthink, and more importantly – discrimination, great leaders must value:
    - Diversity: different people with different ideas, with different backgrounds, who can contribute different value. After all, we are the sum of our parts, so do we really need more of the same? Diversity creates strength.

- Equity: leaders treat others with a sense that they are all equal, regardless of race, gender, age, religious or sexual orientation. Everybody matters.
- Inclusion: rather than 'checking a box' through hiring practices to meet some social obligation, leaders get their teams involved. Through skills like establishing trust and psychological safety that will be discussed in chapter five, great leaders make their teams feel included, and as result, their teams engage and perform!

13. Confidence building: at many times in their career, leaders will find team members under their tutelage with a lot of 'latent potential'. Sometimes, all that a leader needs to do to release some of this stored potential, is to help build a team members' confidence and help them believe in themselves.

We've already established the leadership readiness problem is both massive, and multi-faceted. Let's call it a systemic problem. Systemic issues require systemic solutions, which is why we studied the problem from several vantage points.

As referenced earlier, executive coaches typically (though not always) enter their profession after successful executive careers. They are typically students of the game of leadership, because they often act as teachers and mentors to leaders. We've also established that leaders are being asked to serve, at least some of the time, as coaches to their teams. Here is what the coaches we surveyed had to say about the coaching skills we need to be teaching leaders to set them up for success.

Coaches surveyed: 106

Average years of coaching experience: 11.77

Figure 3.2: Coaches' experience

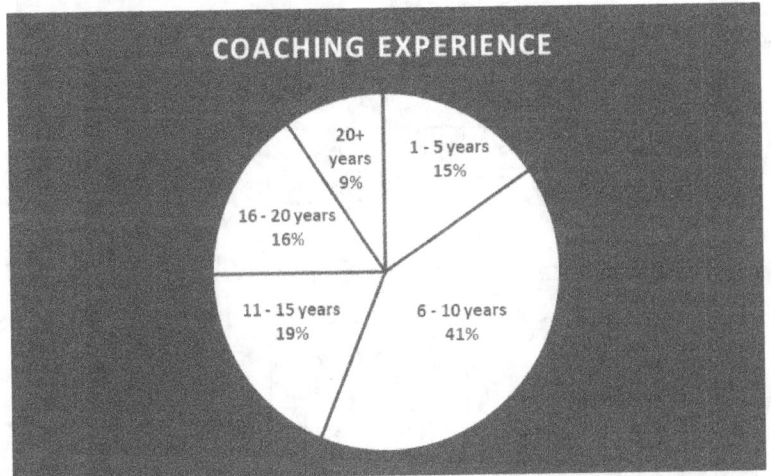

Demographics

Location

Table 3.5: Coaches' geographical distribution

	Country	#	%
1	Canada	21	19.81%
2	UK	20	18.87%
3	United States	10	9.43%
4	Czech Republic	7	6.60%
5	China	5	4.72%
6	Ireland	5	4.72%
7	Poland	3	2.83%
8	France	2	1.89%
9	Germany	2	1.89%
10	Greece	2	1.89%
11	Italy	2	1.89%
12	Malta	2	1.89%
13	The Netherlands	2	1.89%
14	Portugal	2	1.89%
15	Scotland	2	1.89%
16	Australia	1	0.94%
17	Brussels	1	0.94%
18	Cyprus	1	0.94%
19	India	1	0.94%
20	Latin America	1	0.94%
21	New Zealand	1	0.94%
22	Spain	1	0.94%
23	Switzerland	1	0.94%
24	UAE	1	0.94%

Coaching skills raw responses

Table 3.6: Coaching skills raw responses

	What coaching skills must we teach business leaders?	#	%
1	Being a great listener	42	39.62%
2	Empathy	17	16.04%
3	emotional intelligence	13	12.26%
4	Asking profound questions	11	10.38%
T5	Giving and receiving feedback	10	9.43%
T5	Communication skills	10	9.43%
7	Being present	8	7.55%
8	Understanding their currency/ what motivates them	6	5.66%
T9	Creating a safe space	5	4.72%
T9	Being vulnerable	5	4.72%
T9	Build and maintain trust	5	4.72%
T9	Integrity/ honesty/ ethics	5	4.72%
T9	Staying curious	5	4.72%
T9	Self reflection/ reflection skills	5	4.72%
T15	Understanding their values	4	3.77%
T15	Not having to have all the answers/ advice	4	3.77%
T15	Aligning teams' currency to organizational objectives	4	3.77%
T15	Relatability/ building rapport/ relationships	4	3.77%
T15	Help others leverage their strengths	4	3.77%

As you can see when you comb through the coaches' responses, there are no 'technical/ tactical' gaps that made the list. All of the above 19 skills come down to inter-personal skills. Keep in mind that a lot of traditional leadership and management training takes an academic approach: theories in a textbook. Reading theories from a textbook rarely translates into 'soft skill muscle' that leaders can apply at a moment's notice. Table 3.6 below groups the coaches' responses into more of a 'macro-skill' view.

Table 3.7: Coaching skills trends

1 size fits 1 leadership	137
Communication	107
Emotional intelligence	71
Creating alignment	68
Being supportive	68
Leading self	61
Giving and receiving feedback	44
Confidence building	25
Leading through culture	25
Holding others accountable	18
Managing conflict	17

Combining our studies

While both of the above surveys shed light into the leadership problem we were studying, we wanted to see what would happen if we combined all responses into one graph. In other words, if we grew our sample size into 315 responses, we wanted to see if a clear trend emerged from a skill gap basis. The below graph shows a clear trend in terms of the most important skill to prioritize teaching leaders, and also, where leaders, trainers, coaches, and talent development professionals may want to prioritize their resources when it comes to shaping future leaders.

Figure 3.3: Combined Leadership Skill Trends

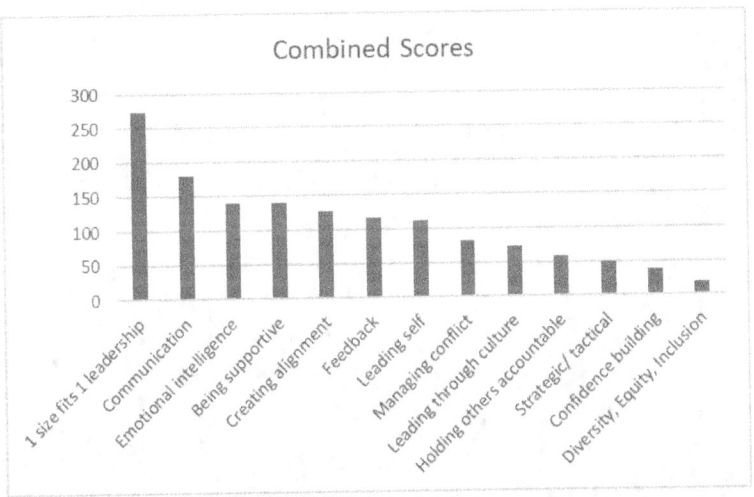

It should go without saying that leadership skill gaps don't just affect the leaders struggling on the job. One study found that one of five employees actually loses sleep due to stress over new managers and how much of a negative impact those ineffectual leaders can have on their work day, if not careers[7].

By now, the picture of the problem has been painted. It's time to shift the focus to what we can do about the problem. The next chapter looks to some of the top leaders in various fields today for inspiration and ideas as to what is working.

4

Beacons of hope

From "13 Days" to "Coach Carter" and "300", there are no shortage of movies that inspire us with moments of great leadership. These classic scenes entertain us, but they also, even if subconsciously, serve as role models – beacons if you will - for what leadership could look like.

Through our research, we dissected the problem thoroughly enough. At least as importantly, we wanted to dive just as deep into solutions. Who better to teach what great leadership entails than those at the very top of the game in their respective fields?

It took several years, but I was fortunate enough to interview some truly world class leaders. I asked these leaders why they got into leadership in the first place, who their role models were, what attributes they feel great leaders must have, and more. I wanted to learn as much as I could, in fact – each of these interviews could have become its own book!

I hope you learn as much as I did, and I sincerely hope I did their words justice! Because each of these leaders is as established as they are, their full biographies are saved for the Appendix section at the end of this book. A high-level summary bio for our leaders is given below.

In alphabetical order, the leaders we interviewed to better understand leadership were;

- Gary Bertwistle. Australian of the year finalist 2018, 3-time TEC speaker of the year, 2-time bestselling author, host of one of the world's most popular podcasts (The Mojo Radio Show, now titled, 'The Mojo Sessions'), and co-founder of the Tour de Cure, Australia's leading

cycling foundation (raised more than $118M for cancer research).
- Nina Bouzamondo-Bernstein. Founder and CEO of Pre-Health Shadowing, an organization of more than 4,700 student volunteers who have helped more than 60,000 pre-health students from around the world gain access to medical, dental, nursing, pharmaceutical and other health shadowing hours. Nina and her team have helped pre-health students earn over 164,000 certificates and designations. Nina is also an advisory board member, women in leadership, at California State Polytechnic University.
- Sister Simone Campbell. Religious leader, attorney, defender of justice, and 2022 recipient of the Presidential Medal of Freedom. Sister Simone Campbell has appeared as a guest on 60 Minutes, The Colbert Report, and The Daily Show with Jon Stewart. She has also received the "Franklin D. Roosevelt Four Freedoms Award" and the "Defender of Democracy Award" from the international Parliamentarians for Global Action.
- Lieutenant-General (LGen) Jennie Carignan. LGen Carignan has served as the Chief, Professional Conduct and Culture for the Canadian Armed Forces since April of 2021. As one of the highest-ranking members of Canada's military, LGen Carignan earned her post through a highly decorated, 36-year career in the Canadian military, including serving as Commander for the NATO Mission Iraq from 2019-2020.
- Ruth Glenn. Ruth is the CEO of the National Coalition Against Domestic Violence and the President of Public Affairs for the National Domestic Violence Hotline. A survivor of domestic violence who shares her experience to help others, Ruth released her memoir, Everything I Never Dreamed, in 2022. Her book became a bestseller

on Amazon, and was featured in several prominent publications, including the Wall Street Journal.
- Nicole Jansen. Expert executive coach with over 30 years' experience as an entrepreneur and coach. Host of the Leaders of Transformation podcast (made the list of the top 50 leadership podcasts in the world 2022), which has over 485 episodes and listeners in more than 140 countries. Nicole is also a sought-after speaker and facilitator who has appeared as a guest on over 90 leadership podcasts or shows.
- Arturo Lomeli. Arturo is the founder of Clase Azul tequila, and the Fundacion Causa Azul. Clase Azul is considered by many experts to be the world's most luxurious tequila. The foundation helps Mexican artisans legitimize their craft and sell their art and creations through proper distribution channels rather than needing to sell on the streets or tourist beaches of Mexico.
- Sonny Melendrez. Often referred to as 'the Dick Clark of San Antonio', Sonny Melendrez is a motivational speaker, radio host, and author. He has been inducted into the rock and roll hall of fame as one of the top 100 radio personalities of all time, as well as the Texas radio hall of fame. Sonny has also appeared in many movies and television roles, from Rocky II and Gremlins, to Fall Guy and The Jetsons. Sonny has helped raise over $100 million dollars for charitable causes over his life, one of the reasons the city of San Antonio named the Sonny Melendrez Community Center after him in 1997.
- Nick Roud. Nick has been recognized as the number one executive coach in all of New Zealand three times. Founder of the leadership coaching company of the year 2022/23 at the Global Business Awards, Nick Roud is one of the world's top executive coaches and a dedicated philanthropist.

- Gene Smith. Senior Vice President and Wolfe Foundation Endowed Athletic Director at THE Ohio State University. Smith is the only person ever to win a Division One football national championship as a player, head coach, and athletic director. Smith oversees almost 500 employees, including a football program the Wall Street Journal valued at $1.5B. Ohio State was recognized by Forbes magazine as "one of the best ten organizations to work for in sports", the only college program on their list. Ohio States' athletes all take part in a unique leadership institute, named after Smith – the Eugene D. Smith Leadership Institute.
- Dr. Marilyn Taylor. Dr. Taylor is a professor of leadership studies at Royal Roads University in Victoria, B.C. There she co-developed the Executive Leadership Specialization MA in Leadership, and was the program head and developer of the Certificate in Values Based Leadership program from 2011 to 2019. Dr. Taylor holds six certifications in culture assessment, organizational psychology, and psychometrics, and has been a university professor for nearly 40 years. Her research in values-based leadership became the catalyst for this book.

Recalling my conversation with Dr. Taylor all those years ago, part of the disconnect between leadership principles and leadership performance was context. It's one thing to recall an academic definition of leadership. It's something entirely different to lead troops into combat like LGen Carignan with lives on the line and everyone looking to her for guidance when they don't know what to do.

In other words, rather than trying to universally define leadership, I wanted to understand its essence from those practicing it at the highest level. Rather than defining leadership,

I wanted our leaders to describe what *living* leadership entailed for them.

What is leadership?

To New Zealand's top executive coach Nick Roud, leadership means "growing others and doing the work that goes unnoticed". For Ohio State Athletic Director Gene Smith, it means "serving in a role, inspiring and motivating others". To Smith, "people are the heart and soul of what we do; the people are all that matters".

Expert executive coach and host of one of the most popular leadership podcasts in the world, Nicole Jansen has a similar view. "Leadership at its essence is influence; inspiring people to be and do more than they would otherwise. Put another way, leadership is guiding people in a direction; giving influence, inspiration, and encouraging action".

Rock and roll hall of fame member and motivational speaker Sonny Melendrez describes leadership as "focusing on a vision and then inspiring others to focus on that same vision". Sonny uses the analogy of a sailor captaining a ship. Only the captain can see where the ship is headed using the ship's telescope, but true leaders are great communicators, and share the view with their team to achieve their buy-in. Leaders must be great communicators, otherwise "it's like trying to box with your hands tied behind your back".

For Clase Azul founder Arturo Lomeli, leadership means "being responsible. Teach with your own example. A boss asks you to do certain things – a leader inspires others to maximize their strengths instead of telling them what to do".

To LGen Jennie Carignan, leadership is about "building, enabling, and creating wealth" (wealth here used interchangeably with 'value'). To LGen Carignan, leaders see teams through a "we are more than the sum of our parts" lens, adding, "the way we do it is as important as what we do". Carignan feels that "leadership is an act of unconditional love. You need to love your team, your organization, and your mission. You need to love your people enough to hear what you don't want to hear, to discipline them when it's time".

To Dr. Marilyn Taylor, leadership means "exercise of influence in the widest possible way". Getting more granular, Dr. Taylor describes personal leadership as "agency, or conscious leadership; being thoughtful and purposeful about what one is doing". In terms of organizational leadership, Taylor is quick to offer "leading people toward a common goal" as her definition, though she adds that leadership can also be leading change.

Sister Simone Campbell takes the notion of leadership to exercise influence or bring about change one step further. To her, leadership is "a means for accomplishing something. For me it's utilitarian; to make change, to get something done, or to protect something. In and of itself, (leadership) doesn't have meaning unless there's an agenda, unless it serves a function."

Sister Campbell points out that "positions (titles) are often seen as leadership, and this is not always the case." Our entire next chapter, in fact, is dedicated to leadership as a set of behaviors, not just titles and organizational structures.

While their experiences are vast and diverse, our leaders align on several important philosophies. It's clear to see the trends above of;

1. Inspiring others to be more and do more
2. Influence over instruction
3. Skillful, if not expert communication
4. Building people and organizations, rather than fighting for a higher portion of finite resources

These are the kind of leaders Greg McKeown and Liz Wiseman were referring to in their 2010 bestseller "Multipliers". These leaders create a multiplier effect within their people and organizations, rather than trying to get the most out of a theoretic ceiling of profit and productivity. They view the world with a lens of abundance, rather than scarcity.

How do great leaders do this? Through intention and attention. Through ideology and through strategy. Let's start with ideology, as in – what ideals or traits must great leaders possess?

The traits of great leaders

Nina Bouzamondo-Bernstein feels that leaders need to be motivated; to "be a doer". As an example, five days after coming up with the concept for Pre-Health Shadowing, Nina had a website up, six subject matter expert speakers booked, content already going out and the platform built. She recognizes that it may have bordered on obsession, and wasn't necessarily a healthy life balance, but it was the only thing she wanted to spend her time on.

Sister Simone Campbell takes 'being a doer' a step further and suggests that leaders need to be willing to take risks. From her perspective, "people tell me I take risks, but I don't feel like they're risks."

Campbell also feels that great leaders are often great storytellers, and they have a way of inviting, if not inspiring, others to become involved. Sister Simone also feels that many great leaders are creative, which would be a critical skill to solving the problem we discussed in chapter two: *we try to teach people to know what to do, when the job is often 'what to do when you don't know what to do'.*

NCADV CEO Ruth Glenn shares that today the world needs more leaders who can see, if not anticipate the "arrows coming at you" (threats) that would affect their organization's values, mission, and capacity. Ruth Glenn reminds us that leaders need to accept, and be prepared for, the reality that threats emerge that weren't accounted for in your strategic plan. You might not be prepared for them, but effective leaders still need to find a way to deal with the unanticipated challenges they are faced with. She points to the global pandemic of 2020 as the quintessential example of the last several years.

LGen Carignan describes the traits of a great leader as collaboration and empathy. You also "need the fortitude and will to push agendas you think are important forward, however there will always be those who need to be convinced, or (seem to resist while they) protect what they value. At the strategic level, not everyone can work for you, many outside your zone of influence have an impact on your mission. You must understand their interests and where they come from, especially when you just wish everyone would do as you say!"

LGen Carignan shares her view that "there is a difference in exercising leadership at the tactical level versus the strategic level. Whether you lead during training exercises, a humanitarian operation, diplomatic missions or combat, leaders need to have a good grasp of the humans conducting the fighting, and understand and adapt to the context."

She shares a powerful example of why empathy is so important. "As your face is full of mud, your boots are wet, in some cases facing an enemy, and you still need to drive forward. In some cases, you've lost people. You need to understand what this all does; these humans need to go back to normal life; to their families after. They need to be able to process what's happening. This was and remains at the top of my mind as a leader".

The military is unique in the sense that there is the very real sense of physical threat that you might not have in the corporate world.

All the aspects of diplomacy still apply in both worlds however, as you need to be able to interact with diplomats. In the military, from combat to peace-keeping, there is a unique challenge in that leaders and their teams travel to host nations with very different cultures. There is a set of tools and leadership skills that you acquire at the junior or tactical level that you can expand or focus on even more as you move to the strategic level.

Sister Simone Campbell shares a similar frame of reference as LGen Carignan, especially her points on empathy. To Campbell, a leader is "someone who listens. Someone who has a strong sense of the needs of others, and is willing to act on (that)."

Campbell adds that leaders have "a maturity; a confidence that isn't swayed by the winds of discord or time." Campbell also mentions that to her, great leaders are strategic.

For New Zealand's top executive coach Nick Roud, leaders must "get comfortable doing the little things consistently well." Roud also shares that in order to ascend to senior leadership positions, "taking stock of your leadership strengths and leadership development areas will enable you to advance in your professional career." Though this reflective practice helps a leader 'climb the ladder', leaders must also look to the future. "The past is done. Get on with your future."

Ohio State Senior Vice President and Athletic Director Gene Smith believes that great leaders must have self-awareness. They must also exhibit a very high EQ (emotional intelligence), even if a leader doesn't always have the highest IQ. Gene also believes great leaders must have the ability to connect with and evaluate others in group settings. Smith adds that the greatest leaders are truly lifelong learners. Finally for Smith, character and integrity are non-negotiables when it comes to leaders. For Smith, leaders must "always be acting from the highest of values".

Dr. Marilyn Taylor argues that knowledge and skill are not enough for leaders today to be successful; they need wisdom. To Taylor, practical wisdom is the capability to make the right decision without knowing everything, and having the courage to find the "real reality". True leaders, suggests Taylor, don't need to be a hero, an expert, or even right. "A leader who needs to be seen as right won't be the leader that's needed in a world that's rapidly and constantly changing". Dr Taylor shares that she struggled to be wise rather than knowledgeable. Taylor reflects that she "was a very poor leader when she had all the answers".

After interviewing (at the time of publication) more than 485 'leaders of transformation', Nicole Jansen has seen a lot of great leadership firsthand. To her, the attributes of a great leader are Influence, inspiration, vision, integrity, discipline, consistency and empathy.

To Arturo Lomeli, the difference between successful and unsuccessful companies is a clear and noble purpose. Arturo succinctly summarizes Clase Azul's purpose, and how it creates a more vibrant and productive workplace. "We exist to captivate the world through the magic of Mexican culture while we transform ourselves into better human beings. Doing that means every single person who paints a bottle every day puts their positive energy into something bigger. We are bigger than just a tequila brand; we are changing the way of leading companies."

In terms of great leadership traits, Gary Bertwistle put it quite succinctly, "*mission* first, not *me* first." Bertwistle adds, "Be intentional. Be where your shoes are. Most people are not intentional, they are reactional. I like to plan my day the night before so that when I get up and go through a morning routine, I'm attacking the day with intention as opposed to rolling over, checking my phone being reactional to everybody else's agenda."

Great leaders bring out the best in others. Sonny Melendrez recalls while filming Rocky II watching Sylvester Stallone play every role; star, writer and director. Sonny shared that not only was Stallone in complete command, but people were also mesmerized by his ability to always get the job done. "As a director, you're at the mercy of the actors, but he always got the shot he wanted, and the performance he wanted out of the actors". As leaders, "directors also need to bring the energy after fatigue sets in for the actors filming scene after scene." Melendrez shares that he's always admired people like Stallone who put themselves into the role they wanted to be in through their work ethic.

Why become a leader in the first place?

In our coaching practice, we've often advised leaders as they began their coaching journey that they were about to run two parallel races in unison. The majority of those leaders signed up to win the long-term race to achieve better results for themselves, their team, and their organization. Most were also surprised to learn they would be running another race; the race with no finish line we call continuous personal development.

To insert another catchphrase, Voltaire famously quoted, "one must cultivate one's own garden". In leadership, this is most certainly the case. It would be downright hypocritical to demand that your team show up early for meetings if you are perennially late. Would you take your boss seriously if they told you how seriously the company values diversity, equity, and inclusion, and then you overheard them utter a racial or homophobic slur while they were on their phone? The culture of any organization – the way people treat one another – starts with the leaders.

Leadership is a responsibility; a duty to uphold for others. It is not an earned title to hold over others or manipulate them with. All of the hard work leaders did to earn the right to lead others simply got them to the start line. Yes, you read that right – the *start line*. Leadership is not a pass to ride on your own coattails and pass on the work to others. Marshall Goldsmith put it best in the title of his bestseller, "What got you here won't get you there".

By no means do we want to turn anyone *away* from leadership; quite the opposite. This book is written to *better prepare as many as possible* for the job that is leadership. That being said, before we go about learning *how* to be a better leader, we must ask *why* anyone would want to be a leader. Leadership, like parenting, can be a thankless job at times. This is exactly why we wanted to ask our leaders their motives for becoming a leader in the first place. We call this their leadership purpose; their 'why' for leading others despite the challenges.

As Richard Barrett points out in The New Leadership Paradigm, a leaders' purpose should involve, to at least some degree, their people.

> *"If you are not passionate about caring for people and you decide to go ahead with becoming a leader, you will need to recognize that your success and the impact you can have on the world will be limited. You will never be a great leader. You may be a good leader, but never great."*[8]

For LGen Carignan, Leadership is important because "it's the ingredient that allows us to be successful in organizing groups of people. We are a weak animal compared to lions. A sheep has more chance to survive alone in the woods, we would probably die of cold on our own. Even with the best talent, you're doomed to fail without great leaders to harness and inspire the full potential of the group. At the State level as an example, we can observe that countries that have everything they need to be successful fail without great leadership".

Carignan cites four reasons for taking on the gravity of leadership responsibility she has in her career.

1. To contribute to something bigger than herself
2. To learn. "I still haven't finished unpacking leadership".
3. Impact. "I have no grand plan of changing the world. Realistically I just like to make a bit of a difference. Manage my expectations and aim to just make a bit of a difference. Some days you feel amazing, and some it's two steps back. As long as you are making progress you are a success".
4. Fourth, it's important to earn a living that also helps others. "If I can't meet all of these objectives through my work, that's when I would look for something else".

Sister Simone Campbell decided to take a position of influence because of an experience in her early social work. She was trying to help with tenants' rights legislation, when "some curmudgeon of a legislator" was asking her about different covenants, and "I didn't know what he was talking about. I hate power imbalance, so I went home and said to the sisters (nuns) I lived with, 'I have to go to law school!'"

Campbell also shares that in high school her younger sister was diagnosed with Hodgkin's disease, and was given three to five years to live. That taught Campbell at a very early age, "how short life is. It was also civil rights, the 1960's (that created) an urgency to get about a sense of justice."

Ruth Glenn opted into leadership because she is a survivor of domestic violence, and is an advocate for survivors. She wanted to help others get out of domestic violence. She couldn't figure out where to put her knowledge of domestic violence, or her passion for ending it, until she saw the position of CEO for the National Coalition Against Domestic Violence (NCADV) pop up. There were looking for, at minimum, an interim director, and Ruth thought she could at least do that. At the time of our interview, that 'interim' was more than 8 years and counting.

Leadership remains so important for Glenn because "there are so many external things driving corporations, not-for-profits and organizations today that it is not a pleasant time". Ruth goes on to share that she's seen a lot of times that external forces in business have been problematic, but that this is a particularly interesting time, calling for "leaders who can recognize what is coming at them". Ruth points to the changing of the American administration (from Obama to Trump) as a time that was challenging for the work that they do. Ruth recalls leadership being like a game of 'whack-a-mole' at the changing of the administration, being pulled in so many directions responding to threats. At times like this organizational effectiveness suffers, says Glenn, as leaders become more reactive than proactive. Ruth is saying the same thing we were – the world has never needed more, better, leaders.

Dr. Marilyn Taylor sees the importance of leadership through a more urgent lens. To Taylor, "It's becoming a crisis situation. Climate change isn't even the biggest global problem, leadership is. We can't deal with climate change unless we have effective leadership doing so".

To Sonny Melendrez, leadership is an act of giving back even while you are receiving support. To Melendrez, "the ladder of success" involves "one arm stretched up to someone who's willing to help you get to the next level and with your other arm, you must be willing to pull someone else up to where you are. It's paying it forward in a way that you're constantly giving back for all the opportunity that you've been given."

In trying to assemble as comprehensive picture of leadership as possible, our interviewees were intentionally chosen from as diverse backgrounds as possible. Hailing from nine different industries, five different countries, and age differences of nearly 50 years, chances are you haven't heard of all of our leaders. Perhaps you haven't heard of any of them, but are inspired by their example. We asked our leaders who inspires them on the world stage of leadership.

Contemporary leadership examples

According to LGen Carignan, "there are very few revolutions throughout history that have been successful. The American Revolution is one example that worked because of the leadership of George Washington, because of the type of person he was".

Carignan points out Nelson Mandala as another example. "He had his flaws, we can't expect everyone to be perfect, but was a unifying force at a critical moment in South Africa's history even after spending 27 years in prison". Angela Merkel is who LGen Carignan would most like to meet. Merkle, to Carignan is "a very humble, visionary and values-based leader; 16 years leading a very complex place like Germany".

Finally for Carignan, Marcus Aurelius. She took a lot from his book "Meditations", specifically, how to approach leadership from a military point of view.

Sister Simone Campbell highlights the work of Margit Slachta, the first female member of the Hungarian parliament, as well as one of the founders of the Sisters of Social Service. She also mentions Nancy Pelosi, whose superpower to Campbell is listening and remembering people. To Simone, Nancy Pelosi remembers connections and is able to create a unity and direction in very turbulent times. She also creates space for other people's vision(s). Campbell remembers sharing this with Pelosi, who laughed and quipped, "well, I am a mother of five – I have a lot of people to remember!"

To Nicole Jansen, the world leaders (past and present) who most exemplify values-based leadership are Jesus Christ, Nelson Mandela, Mahatma Gandhi, Abraham Lincoln, Mother Theresa, coach John Wooden, David Green founder of Hobby Lobby, and John Maxwell, who asserts that leadership is more about building other leaders than followers. Many more values-based leaders will never be found in history books, but are found impacting lives wherever they go. Values matter.

Gene Smith credits his father, an electrician with five employees when Gene was growing up, as the source of much of his leadership wisdom. Gene worked construction with his dad and his team growing up, and never forgot their attention to detail. No 'little thing' was too small not to be taken seriously or professionally. Later, Gene attributes a lot of his early leadership influence and example to Ara Parseghian, the legendary Notre Dame Football coach whom Gene played for.

NCADV CEO Ruth Glenn has modeled much of her leadership style after former President Barack Obama. She feels he's a great orator. He is also full of passion that inspires belief, hope and conviction in others. "He built an alliance of people who believed we could do better. That always stuck with me".

Dr. Marilyn Taylor lists a few contemporary leaders as being particularly values-based;

- Former U.S. President Barack Obama: To Dr. Taylor, he exemplifies a certain grace, even though he's endured a lot of racism and political push-back.
- German Chancellor Angela Merkel: To Taylor, Merkel assumed her role as a dedicated person to her country. She didn't play a hero in the way she dealt with it, and

she dealt with complex situations like the German immigration issue.
- Canadian Prime Minister Justin Trudeau: To Dr. Taylor, Trudeau has "assembled an amazing array of advisors who he actually listens to, and is not afraid to push against opposition to do what he feels is right".
- Ed Clark with TD Bank. According to Taylor, when working with a multi-national bank it's very challenging due to the sheer size and the number of regulations, but he created a very different culture compared to their industry counterparts. "Do not worry about your job, that is not how we're going to solve this problem" was a critical message from Clark to the entire company in 2009 amidst fears of job security.

When explaining her choices above, Dr. Taylor elaborates that leadership on the world stage is always measured against context (war, societal shifts, disaster, etc). Political leaders especially, are rarely popular in real time but often measured after their tenure by the ability to affect needed change.

To Sonny Melendrez, anyone who is philanthropic is a great example of a leader. He feels we should aspire to be more like people who give back, even if we've never heard of them

It came as no surprise that our interviewees would share a few leaders (Mandala, Obama, Merkel) in common. As stated in the introduction - everyone knows great leadership when they see it, but can anyone define it? We can recognize, and even agree on, great leadership. So how do we understand it enough to help build better leaders for the future?

My mentor and business partner Matt Young's adage is that leaders should leave those in their care better than they found them. Whether our team members work for us for a day or a decade, they should be better off in some way, shape, or form because of us.

Leaving people better off than you found them requires care. It requires an investment in people over and above the job description. Sometimes this takes the form of mentorship. Sometimes it's sharing your own lived experience to help others achieve similar success in less time. Sometimes it's as simple as asking your team how they're doing and actually caring about their answer. Caring is a segue into core values, the 'moral compass' or ethical code a leader lives by. As you'll read ahead, great leaders are clear on their core values.

Values in action

Arturo Lomeli defines the notion of leadership values in action. His greatest source of pride comes not from winning so many 'tequila of the year' awards, or being offered $1B for his company[9]. For Arturo, it's "our people, definitely. We are a family with the best people. We are happy; we work in the path of values. We look towards humanity, justice, freedom. This is not a kingdom; this is a beautiful company where every single person counts. We don't use numbers, we use names".

What's amazing about those famous white-with-blue-flowers tequila bottles, is that even though more than 50,000 cases of them ship every year, every single one is hand crafted and hand painted in the small village of Santa Maria Canchesda. As it is with every ingredient of their fine tequilas, each ingredient in building the business to what it is today was a careful and intentional decision. Arturo was originally employing a local artisan by the name of Tomas to create the trademark Clase Azul bottles. As demand grew, the two men realized that Clase Azul accounted for 90% of Tomas' capacity in the small shop adjacent to his house! This led to a critical decision; ship production to China for a fraction of the price, or do something bold to invest in keeping jobs in Mexico. Despite Arturo's recollection that neither of the men had any money to invest – they decided to jointly open a new factory in Santa Maria. At the time of our interview this factory employed 120 of the towns' inhabitants, a significant percentage of the local workforce.

Further evidence of Arturo's commitment to his community and the local economy came in the development that 80% of his employees at the factory were women. A great majority of Mexican men would relocate to the United States to find higher paying jobs. With so many women in the workforce, time away from work due to pregnancy and raising small children was a major issue both for the families and their income, and the factory and its production. This led Arturo and his team to begin offering childcare, which they now do with a capacity for 70 kids!

Arturo refers to the families working for him to as a family. The employees in the local town making Clase Azul receive breakfast and lunch – free. Lomeli and his team found that even raising pay for the families did not help educate them on the importance of proper nutrition. In a very small village like Santa Maria Canchesda, health education and healthy meal options are not always universally available, nor a priority for the typically poor families living there. By implementing a breakfast and lunch program – Arturo and his team were having a direct impact on the health of their working family and their community.

Gary Bertwistle recalls one of his greatest lessons in values from his first guest on The Mojo Sessions, Dr. John Demartini. "What do you value most in life, and what are your actions demonstrating?" "It's not about how much time, but if friends and connection is something you value the most, it could be a loving text, a quick phone call, or sending a card. It could take 60 seconds but your actions demonstrate that you are executing upon the things that you value the most as opposed to just talking about it and getting busy".

Sister Simone Campbell shares a powerful compass guiding her leadership actions. When faced with challenges or opportunities, she asks herself and her team, "how do we use this moment for mission?"

In describing her mission, Campbell refers to part of the Catholic 'vow formula'; "to live and love for the Lord Jesus Christ. For me this is about trying to weave together community in a very disparate country."

Sister Campbell has found herself at two pivotal moments in her career on the side of the minority on polarizing issues. Though she was personally thanked by President Barack Obama for her support of the affordable care act, the U.S. Conference of Catholic Bishops was publicly opposed to the act. Campbell was also attentioned by Pope Benedict XVI for her supposed "radical feminist themes incompatible with the Catholic faith", though this investigation was ended by Pope Francis in 2015[10].

In these moments, Sister Campbell shares that she defers to the "prophetic imagination that Walter Brueggemann talks about", and one of his key teachings that leaders ought to "touch the pain of the world as real." Campbell shares the story of how she kept the picture of a young woman who lost her job during the recession and had no health care. This young woman was diagnosed with colon cancer, and ended up dying of cancer, even though it was treatable. "I've carried her picture for 10 years now as the story of *why* people should have access to health care – it's a right".

For Sister Campbell, leaders can become disconnected if "they aren't close enough to the pain of the world. This is what Pope Francis means when he talks about 'encounter'". When these leaders are so removed that they start to act to the detriment of their people, Sister Campbell feels it's the responsibility of other leaders to "struggle against them. Do what you can and put out an alternative view."

For all of the work she has done, and all of her accomplishments, Sister Simone simply laughed when I asked if she thought more about what's been accomplished, or what's left to be done, then confirmed, "clearly (I focus more on) what's left to accomplish!"

Sonny Melendrez lives by the credo "every Friday night when your head hits the pillow and you review the past week, ask yourself 'were you a good father? Were you a good husband? Were you a good steward, helping others?"

Nicole Jansen is very intentional about honoring her word with herself and others. "If I'm not going to do it, I won't say it". Jansen observes that even with something as conversationally trivial as 'let's do lunch', we tend to use our words so flippantly, and we can lose credibility in the process. A few of her podcast guests have preached not to be flippant with their words; "this causes us to be out of integrity, and an incongruence between words and actions is not true leadership, whether in business or in life". In seeking to become 100% congruent inside and out, Nicole learned to not say anything that she does not absolutely mean.

Lomeli also believes it is critical to be impeccable with his words. "People get much more involved because of this example and the synergy of the team is much higher", says Arturo. He goes on to implore leaders, "instead of controlling people, give them freedom to do their best. If they make a mistake, a leader can explain why the perspective can be different next time."

Perhaps because our leaders are so focused on their team, and so humble, it comes as no surprise that our leaders have learned a lot from their teams.

Lessons from their teams

LGen Jennie Carignan says she has learned a tremendous amount from her team. "Sure, you're the boss, but you can always put yourself in a position where you're willing to learn from (your team). This is where you get to learn about your leadership style and the impact you have on others. That exchange can happen if you're open to it". For many of the leaders we've coached, this is a rare and beautiful gift. Most leaders don't get feedback in real time, and are too busy, and need guidance in ascertaining their 'leadership brand'. Unless they work with a coach and have completed a 360-degree review*, many leaders simply don't know what kind of leader they are, how they're doing, or how they're 'showing up'.

"Your folks will 'poke' a bit to see if it works (a true exchange), and if not, they're not going to try again" Carignan adds.

It's important for senior leaders to recognize that some team members aren't comfortable speaking up, or speaking candidly about their challenges, for fear of retribution. At these times, warns Carignan, it's important to 'set the stage', create a safe space for exchanges, model the behavior, and let the team know that you want their feedback and/ or opinion.

She also had one of her team members tell her, "it's okay to be yourself." In other words, you don't need to be 'on all the time' as a leader. That comment also helped LGen Carignan know early that she was "probably not as authentic as I thought I was being". LGen Carignan admits she learned a lot from her kids too.

(*a 360-degree review is a collection of surveys with a leaders' most relevant stakeholders. This is usually direct supervisors, peers, and direct reports, but may include previous employers/ peers, long-term customers or suppliers, and even the leaders' significant other)

Dr. Marilyn Taylor may not have direct reports like the rest of our leaders, but she is curious and humble enough to learn a lot from her students. One such lesson: "going with what's possible rather than what's ideal; sometimes even – what's better than my ideal. As long as people are doing work that has integrity, and in their view is the best thing to be doing; there are a lot of different ways to learn".

Professor Taylor shares that her students have also helped teach her flexibility and openness to differences. She admires so many of them. Taylor shares she has been fortunate to have some of the best leaders in her classes over the years, and they have shown her "just how exquisite great leadership can be".

On what her clients and podcast guests have taught her about leadership over the years, Nicole Jansen is quickly filled with gratitude. "I've learned so much from my podcast guests over the years! I've learned the 'language of leadership'. I've learned that questions lead, and answers follow". Finally, Nicole is grateful to have learned the importance of empathy; the beautiful blend of power and empathy in influencing people to action.

New Zealand's top executive coach Nick Roud is much the same. He shares feeling deep gratitude, even luck, to have worked with the leaders he has over the years, and to have learned as much as he has from them. This from a coach who has a 'you get results or you get your money back' guarantee.

Sister Simone Campbell shares the gift of self-awareness her team gave her. The toughest piece of feedback she ever received from her team was that she was not a spiritual leader. Imagine hearing that as a nun! Campbell shares that her reflective practice was essential to being able to grow from this feedback. "You sit with the pain until you know the truth. The only reason criticism hurts is because there's some truth to it. I came to realize that I was a spiritual leader, but my fellow sisters didn't see it. I didn't reveal that part of myself. The big change for me was the willingness to share my spiritual journey. That insight has led me to who I am now, but it was my sisters who taught me to speak it."

The greatest lesson Gene Smith says his team has taught (or reminded) him over the years is to stay humble; to stay who you are. This, says Smith has allowed him to stay sensitive to the needs of the team. Smith also learns from adversity. The greatest lesson Gene Smith says he's learned through failure or adversity is around decision making. Smith talks about the "Mood Elevator", and how the quality of our decisions is linked to our emotional state. The best time to make decisions, Smith says, is when we feel good. Ohio State's Vice President and Athletic Director admits he's made decisions when frustrated or upset, which he's worked to change over the years.

Sonny Melendrez has organized a Christmas toy drive every year since 2001. He shares that the inspiration for the toy drive, came from a couple of five-year-olds at San Antonio Academy. These five-year-old boys asked their parents what they could do when they learned that some children go without toys or even food at Christmas. Ever since, the annual toy drive has arranged hundreds of toys for less fortunate children in the San Antonio area, and it all started with what these five-year-old boys taught him.

Melendrez shares that he has always had an innate desire to give back, which he learned well before leading teams. "I get that from my mom. She was always helping someone." Sonny feels honored that in his career he's "been able to connect the haves with the have-nots". Many times, the have-nots are the ones giving, says Sonny, like the 1997 Guadalupe River flood in San Antonio. One woman for instance, took three buses to get to the fundraiser Sonny organized, to donate a toothbrush and toothpaste because that's what she could afford. To Sonny, "we are never happier than when we are in the service of others".

From traits to tactics

We've looked at our great leaders from many angles; from their values and philosophies to their definition of leadership. Now how do we put these concepts into action? How do we go from quotable quotes to measurable (and desirable) results? How have these leaders made sure that the 'rubber hit the road' to accomplish all that they have?

For example, how did Gene Smith and his team of coaches and administrators create such success in one of the most cutthroat industries on the planet? Smith shares that his team took a very Jim Collins (Good to Great) approach. It was all about getting the right people in place. In fact, Smith spent his first year as Ohio State's Athletic Director evaluating the athletic departments' culture and people. He looked at every position. He looked at the organizational goals and objectives. From there he developed a performance management plan. Smith taught his team how to be evaluated, and how to evaluate others. More importantly says Smith, the leadership team created platforms for communication.

So called 'management' began to revolve around professional and personal goals, rather than just wins and losses or on-field performance. Smith and his team led with the philosophy of always asking "how can we help?" as opposed to micromanagement or only focusing on their direct reports' deliverables.

Smith is clear in outlining that they were very intentional to demonstrate care in formal and informal evaluations. By leading with care, Smith admits, it made adding the accountability needed to drive a high-performance culture infinitely easier. This approach made its way from Ohio States' electricians to their ground crew to marketing and of course, their coaches and players.

On a more operational level within his direct control, Smith shared his focus (at the time of our interview) on the 12 people in his department who could jump into major leadership positions very soon. Most won't be at Ohio State, which speaks to the true people-centric leadership stance Smith has taken. "Develop people so well that you lose some of them", he said. As the timing of these positions starts to open, Smith always wants to have an honest conversation because he never wants any teammate bumping against the ceiling, feeling like there's no room for growth. He gives them options, even if this includes leaving.

Smith wants to make sure that for whoever follows him, whenever that day comes, that the program is in the greatest of health. In other words, Smith wants to leave Ohio State better than he found it. Just like he has every student, athlete, coach, janitor, and Buckeye fan and staff member he has touched. Smith was nearing his retirement at the time of publication, and by all accounts he has left Ohio State better than he found it in a great many ways.

To Dr. Marilyn Taylor, the mindset one chooses when leading is the difference between 'values-based' leadership and conventional leadership. This includes, but is not limited to, letting team members know what's expected from them, proper remuneration, and maintaining a safe environment. To Taylor, top level leaders are bound to their organizations through common values and a common mission. They create a clear line of sight to what each team member is doing and what the teams' mission is. Great leaders, says Taylor, create organizations that are self-regulating in how the team adjusts to meet goals. That is, the expectations and outcomes are clear, but the pathways are often more autonomous and collaborative.

The above 'self-regulation' with respect to the organization is a mark of its' culture. Though culture can be defined in many ways, perhaps Taylor's simplest explanation is "the way things are done around here". The culture of an organization, argues Taylor, determines its' ultimate success in that "leaders can make all the changes they want to in terms of business processes, but it won't make a difference if those changes don't align with the underlying culture. If you don't match the DNA in an organ transplant, the tissue will likely be rejected. Culture is much the same".

Because culture is dictated by leadership, the traits and values of an organizations' leaders are critical. As Dr. Taylor puts it, "the leaders' values become the organizations' values". As such, it is critical that all leaders have an engaged understanding of their own impact on the culture. Leaders must walk the talk – making sure what they say they value actually aligns with their actions. As Dr. Taylor puts it, "one should not even mention the word values in relation to leadership unless they're willing to walk the talk". To Taylor, this requires understanding, vulnerability, and the will to hear and explore "what I didn't know that I didn't know".

The detail and purpose behind every decision the team at Clase Azul makes is central to their belief that everything they do ends up as greater product quality. Every investment in their people ends up as higher product quality for their customers.

Per his philosophy to create value and be different, the team at Clase Azul took a different approach to build their brand. "We were not just selling, we were teaching; captivating – sharing the knowledge with bar owners, managers, bartenders – the passion of tequila". Sharing knowledge paid off because they didn't see other brands as competitors – more like everyone gets to experience the quality difference because Clase Azul doesn't cut any corners. They compete with quality and honesty. "We are not in a rush. We have no investors". In other words, there was no need to provide quarterly shareholder returns, which has allowed Arturo and his team to take a long-term view in terms of their market position, strategy, and how they define success.

To Arturo Lomeli, it's far more important to invest in people and focus on your company's impact than it is just to make short term profit decisions. Today, Clase Azul employs over 200 people and Arturo sees this as his leadership responsibility. They ended up building their own grid-neutral factory. They run all operations such that they produce their own energy, or add to the energy grid. The facility is 100% green. Lomeli concedes that doing things this way can cost more, but this is the example they want to set for other businesses and future generations.

"We provide the best benefits because we believe that it's our responsibility as entrepreneurs and leaders of the company to take care of our employees, and they will take care of the company."

The same care extends even in the face of evil. Ruth Glenn believes it's essential that the work her and the teams at NCADV and NDVH are doing is done "with a survivor's voice at the center of it. A survivor can be a leader. As a leader, I also bring my story, and I'm going to tell you my story, because I'm not doing this for the money. I'm doing it so that you understand, and so you join the effort."

Ruth's comments underpin an essential leadership trait – vulnerability. Sharing our vulnerability as leaders creates emotional connections with our team, and a commitment to more than a paycheck. This is how great leaders inspire the commitment from their team that they would 'run through a brick wall' for their leader.

In order to stay positive in an industry full of rejection, and with a dark side of narcissism, substance abuse, and impossible standards, Sonny Melendrez focuses on seeing the bigger picture, and remaining optimistic. "I don't believe in miracles; I rely on them". To Sonny, it's also important to consider attitude, "there's always a way to get to where you want to go if you keep the right frame of mind." It's also important to put in the work to get better at your craft. He even has a rhyme he recites; "every day before you play, do three things that will further your goal." Sonny's logic is that following this framework leads to "planting 720 seeds every year".

Sonny Melendrez also advocates for networking to create the success you want in your career. The two-time Billboard Magazine presenter of the year reminds us that "it's show business, not 'hide' business". Surround yourself with like-minded people: "people who have vision; people who are in tune with the joy of life". Remember "you are always being watched, so be somebody who is worth watching."

For Nina Bouzamondo-Bernstein, "leadership has shifted, listening is a big part of leadership". When she started out Nina viewed leadership more as management, "how am I setting things up, how am I going to have everyone execute? Now it's more of what do people need? Inspiration, motivation, and an ear. Providing a platform for others to do what they feel is best".

LGen Carignan echoes a very similar sentiment, "we tend to promote great tacticians, however the skills needed at the next level are often very different than those that helped them excel". To be so bold, one could argue that management and leadership are completely different skills – possibly even unrelated skills. This helps shed some light on why many leaders fail – we might be promoting based on the wrong criterion.

It's important for Nina to take a leadership position in life because she feels like she was given so much. "With that privilege comes great responsibility." Not everyone has access to what I've had access to. We live in an inequitable society. That's something that is horrible that I would love to change. I'm a white woman in America, I want to share resources to be able to help the most amount of people in the most beneficial way". In fact, Nina's LinkedIn header picture has the words, "I am for equity because equity starts with everyone."

While she may be a very supportive leader, Nina also has highly transparent expectations, from email turnaround times to service delivery. When you give people more autonomy and clarity, they own up to it. They don't want to let anybody down. Nina sees this empowerment, this increase in autonomy, as a direct reason her organization now sees less turnover and greater productivity. Ruth Glenn adds," I pride myself on making my team feel valuable, that they belong. This is their work, they own this".

To Sister Simone Campbell, one fundamental she feels is essential for leaders like Nina to evolve as described above is some form of reflective practice. For her, it's a contemplative practice, but she feels all leaders need some form of reflection that helps shape their perspective, and "allows for surprising insight."

Gary Bertwistle reminds us that nothing great happens by accident. Intentionality and routine are essential for leaders according to Gary, an expert in creativity and innovation. He cites Da Vinci to make his point, "there's no room in the busy mind for creativity". Key for Bertwistle is intentionality. He argues that "most of us are not intentional, we are reactional".

To make effective decisions, and achieve consistently positive results, leaders must surround themselves with those better, smarter, or differently wise. Nina Bouzamondo-Bernstein has a mentor, a board of advisors, and a team who brings knowledge she doesn't necessarily have to the table. She also credits her father as her biggest supporter who challenged her to go after her idea for her startup when many others (trying to protect her from failure) told her not to.

I've lost track of how many times I've poured over these interviews, trying to do their wisdom the justice it deserves. Each of these interviews deserves to be its' own book, however, the leadership problem we've discussed cannot wait any longer for a solution.

Upon contemplating the wisdom of our 11 great leaders, let us remember these 13 lessons;

1. Great leaders are driven by a profound purpose, an inspiring vision, and are uncompromising in living in alignment with their values.
2. Flowing from their vision, leaders are intentional. They act, speak, and even think with intention, as Gary Bertwistle models. "Just because" or "that's how we've always done it" are not phrases you'll hear from a great leader. Being a visionary carries a unique set of challenges, and so Dr. Marilyn Taylor warns, "Don't lose the idea if you're too early to market or experiencing challenges with its reception".
3. In addition to intention, leaders exemplify focus. Time management is a challenge for all leaders, and there is always more work to do than time to do it. For these reasons, great leaders know how to prioritize their agenda, and stay focused on what matters most in the moment.
4. Leadership is a duty born out of service, not a position of power one becomes entitled to.
5. Great leaders are focused on potential, and committed to leaving people and organizations better than they found them.

6. Great leaders are also focused on their stakeholders (fans, customers, clients, students). Even for one of the most popular sports organizations on the planet, Gene Smith of Ohio State feels "You've got to build the brand one fan at a time".
7. Great leaders give their team autonomy, and inspire a sense of ownership.
8. Caring about the team is non-negotiable, even "an act of unconditional love" as LGen Jennie Carignan put it.
9. Great leaders are not selfish, but they are consistently focused on self-improvement. To Arturo Lomeli, "You never get to the end. You never achieve your maximal potential. Always be aware, learning, moving forward. You get to the point you know everything the day you die".
10. Great leaders are humble enough to admit their mistakes, and wise enough to try and learn from every mistake they make.
11. Great leaders take action. They are 'doers' as Nina Bouzamondo-Bernstein put it.
12. Great leaders are committed to the vision, but agile in their approach. They need to anticipate the "arrows coming at you" as NCADV CEO Ruth Glenn shared.
13. Great leaders are passionate. Repeating Arturo Lomeli's words, "We exist to captivate the world through the magic of Mexican culture while we transform ourselves into better human beings."

One major trend I've intentionally not attributed to any individual leader interviewed is where their leadership came from. I mentioned earlier asking these titans of leadership who their mentors were. The biggest surprise of this entire project for me, was how few of these world class leaders actually had one. An alarming trend was just how many of our leaders had no great leader to model themselves after. While some of our leaders had brilliant examples of effective, ethical leadership to model, more than I would have guessed were simply trying to become the kind of leader they wished they had coming up.

The silver lining to this shocking revelation, if I may offer it, is that anyone can become a leader. You are not barred from consideration just because you didn't go the right school, or learn from a leadership guru. If you care enough about your people, and you care enough to put in the time to learn, and you care enough to improve, you can become a great leader. Thinking back to my views on leadership when I first started leading a team, I find that to be a great relief, even inspiring in a way.

Our next chapter moves from inspiration to implementation. Our great leaders have painted an inspiring picture of what could be. Now the $366 billion dollar question is: how do we do that? How do we do that consistently, and learn to teach others? Our next chapter breaks down 'one size fits one leadership' into 15 bite-size, teachable skills.

5

One size fits one leadership

In July of 2023, I conducted a poll with my LinkedIn network. I asked those in leadership why they choose to work in leadership. In order of popularity, their responses were;

1. Wanting to coach or mentor others – 70.59%
2. I need a team in order to reach my vision – 11.76%
3. It's my job; no one else will do it – 5.88%

While this is just one poll, the trends are very clear: most leaders get into, or stay in leadership, to help others more than just to achieve personal gain or corporate objectives. This is a very important motive to remember when we teach leadership, and what skills we prioritize teaching leaders. As most leaders are well aware, time spent learning leadership, or any other skill, is time spent away from the business. There is a financial cost to leadership training, but there is also an opportunity cost to the leaders' time. Most businesses simply cannot afford their leaders being away for too long a period of time. Leaders need to prioritize what they want to learn, and coaches and trainers must prioritize what they teach to maximize impact, and minimize this opportunity cost.

Earlier, we mentioned how leaders are running two races in unison; one for results through bettering their team, and an endless race of personal and professional betterment. As John Maxwell put it in his book LeaderShift, "there is no finish line when it comes to improving, and there is no complete picture of leadership that can be mastered[11]." While there is no finish line, the start line of this race is self-awareness.

The more aware a leader is of their emotions, triggers, and stressors, the more they can exercise self-control, and emotional management techniques. For Gene Smith, "leaders must know themselves, and then exercise strong self-management, before attempting to lead others". Smith feels that what he and his leadership team at Ohio State have done well; "creating the shadow of a leader". That is, they all behave in a way that people know what's expected of them. Ohio State leaders "lead by example, and demonstrate their values through their actions more than through their speech".

Furthermore, increased self-awareness allows a leader to be more present for their team. This is one of the central skills of any effective coach, and we've already made the case for how leaders need to be coaches for their team in today's organization.

Self-awareness is also essential for effective decision-making. As Jeanne Segal points out in The Language of Emotional Intelligence, high stress levels make us emotionally unavailable and keep us "trapped in our own heads"[12]. In this sense, self-awareness is an ongoing objective, not a 'box to check' or mountain to climb once. It's always important.

The more aware and present we are, the more effective we are as leaders. Self-awareness can be achieved in several ways;

1. Self-reflection
2. Feedback from others
3. Taking inventory of your thoughts, beliefs, behaviors and performance on a regular basis
4. Acquiring and practicing new skills, based on the above

As we begin to cultivate greater self-awareness, one of the first and most important places for us to direct it is our mental attitude. Our attitude – the way we choose to see and react to the world – is one of the most important choices we can make in life. It's a choice we make countless times every day of our lives.

We choose our attitude when we react to the weather outside. We choose our attitude when we are met with a traffic jam on the way to work. We choose our attitude every time we interact with other people, and we choose our attitude every time we get news we weren't hoping or expecting to hear. We choose our attitude when our team loses the firm's biggest client, and we must face the board of directors to explain our third quarter earnings shortfall.

We believe our attitude lives on a spectrum; several, in fact. In the most general sense, you choose a good attitude or a bad attitude. We prefer to think of this more as the 'victim or victor' spectrum. You can choose to be a victim, blaming everyone and everything else for why things aren't turning out the way you'd hoped. You can choose to be a 'victor', and rise above any adversity or challenge laid in front of you. You cannot choose both at the same time. In any moment, in any situation, on this spectrum you are either a victim, or a victor. You are victorious… or you aren't.

Similar to the 'victim or victor' spectrum, leaders can choose to look at life through a 'scarcity or abundance' attitude. An attitude of scarcity might lead you to take a high potential's resignation personally. You might feel like they are abandoning you, and 'good employees are so hard to find'. An attitude of abundance would choose to celebrate the occasion, because it's good for them that they found another opportunity, it's good for the team because someone else now needs to step up, and it's good for the business because you now have another advocate out there saying great things about your company in the marketplace. We could go on, but we think you get the picture. We've already established that great leaders think in terms of abundance. Recall

Gene Smith's philosophy, "develop people so well that you lose some of them".

If our attitude is a choice, the options we have available to us are an extension of our focus. Our focus is what we chose to see, and where we choose to exert our attention and energy. Victims focus on problems. Victors focus on solutions and opportunities. Those with an attitude of scarcity focus on what others have, and they almost always compare with those who have more. Those with an abundance attitude focus on gratitude. They are grateful for what they have, and for the opportunity to achieve more and help others do the same.

Sonny Melendrez's first job in radio was while he was still a student in El Paso, TX. He would be on the air from 5:00am until noon on Sundays, more than twice as long as the average radio host's show. Sonny's attitude was always "oh good, I still have four hours left". How many others in this situation would be exasperatedly thinking "oh man, I *still* have four hours left"? To this day, Sonny shares he maintains an "oh good, I still have..." attitude.

No matter how early in the game you are, or how far you go; as a leader you will always have three key decisions in front of you before you lead even one more person.

1. How am I showing up? This is the self-awareness question. A leader can assess how they are 'showing up' with respect to their effort level, whether or not they are being triggered or potentially triggering others, or simply if they feel *'on'* or not for the big presentation. It's also a key question to leading self, one of the key skills identified in our survey in chapter three.
2. What attitude am I choosing in this moment? This is the empowerment question; will you be a victim or a victor?

Will you see the opportunities around you as limited or limitless?

3. What am I focused on? This is the fulfillment question. Are you choosing to see problems, or looking for solutions? Are you robbing yourself of joy by focusing on those who seem to have more than you? Are you creating joy by focusing on all of the good already present in your life?

Welcome to your endless race. There may be no finish line, but that doesn't mean there are no winners. The more you choose your attitude and focus, the more fulfilling and abundant your life will be. The more you invest in your own leadership education and performance, the more winners there will be in your team and in your life. The better you lead yourself, and those around you, the more far-reaching and long-lasting your leadership legacy will be. What an opportunity!

Now, as a leader, you already know that leadership is not about you, so we now turn our attention to the race our team is running, and how you as their 'leader coach' can help them enjoy more victories. As you learn fifteen essential coaching skills from some of the world's top executive coaches, it's important to keep in mind that these skills are interrelated.

While we are not trying to universally define leadership once and for all, perhaps it is useful to think of great leadership as a symphony, in which the individual players (micro-skills) contribute to create a harmony wherein the sum is greater than the total of its parts.

Chapter three defined 'one size fits one' leadership as the most in-demand, and most ill-prepared skill for leaders today. As we break down each component skill of 'one size fits one' leadership, don't lose sight of the forest for the trees. It's important to learn the component skills, but also why each is important as they contribute to the more multi-faceted skills we are trying to master.

Alex Pascal, Founder of Coaching.com, shared with me in an email the key coaching skills for both executive coaches and leaders to focus on for 2023 and beyond. According to Coaching.com, these skills are;

1. Adaptability
2. Communication
3. Agility
4. Listening
5. Flexibility
6. Powerful questioning
7. Critical thinking

As you'll see through the rest of this chapter, the 15 skills our survey identified are very similar.

Our skills are listed in a sequential order of sorts. Each skill lends itself to the next. While there is not necessarily a hierarchy of these skills, the first skill is not only chronologically first for many reasons, it just might be the most important for all leaders to learn.

Skill One: *Create a safe space*

While the skills covered in the next fifteen sections will be dedicated to who you serve (we choose to see leadership as a position of service), it's important to consider the nature of interactions you will have with your team. Is the physical and emotional environment you will be interacting with your team conducive to a productive and mutually beneficial relationship? In coaching terms, have you created a safe space for your team?

While physical security may be an issue in some workplaces (just ask LGen Carignan), what we're really talking about here is the level of psychological safety your team feels at work. The first task of the leader is to create an environment in which their team is comfortable coming to them with their questions, challenges, and ideas. As NCADV CEO Ruth Glenn puts it, "leaders need to create a safe space where mistakes can be admitted, it helps the workforce operate better".

Creating a safe space is not just the first order of business, this is also the most important skill in this entire framework. No matter how great a leader may be, they will only get part of the story if their team doesn't feel safe and able to trust their leader at all times. We'll never get the opportunity as leaders to coach our team to step into their potential if we don't nail this first piece of the puzzle. Believe it or not, your subconscious mind is constantly on the lookout for danger, scanning your environment five times a second for threats![13]

According to the Center for Creative Leadership, organizations can take eight steps to fostering an environment of psychological safety in the workforce[14];

1. Make psychological safety an explicit priority
2. Facilitate everyone speaking up
3. Establish norms for how failure is handled
4. Create space for new ideas (even wild ones)
5. Embrace productive conflict
6. Pay close attention and look for patterns
7. Make an intentional effort to promote dialogue
8. Celebrate wins

One of the best ways an individual leader can achieve a safe space is to lead with vulnerability. Leaders share first. In my fitness career, I used to think the team wanted direction on how to get from 'point A' to 'point B' in their careers. I'd been in their shoes, and had become a manager, owner, and local public figure in the fitness industry. When I shared success tips, career hacks, and that I wanted to help them get to 'the next level' – the results were mixed at best.

When I started sharing my story – screw-ups, mistakes, and the hard times – with every new recruit, the results were astonishing. The commitment, loyalty, and quality of relationships and trust created were unlike anything I'd experienced before.

NCADV CEO Ruth Glenn takes creating a safe space through sharing and being vulnerable to a whole new level. Survivor of domestic violence, Ruth shared her story in her bestseller, "Everything I Never Dreamed: My life surviving and standing up to domestic violence". It's her personal account of her story, and for Ruth, "I want to exude how important it is to end domestic violence. I want you to *feel* that. I don't want to just talk about it."

Ruth's powerful example notwithstanding, in no way am I suggesting you 'jump into the deep end' and over-share, or share deeply personal facts and stories before you are ready. Let your personal core values, your boundaries, and your comfort zone with personal sharing be your guide. Keep in mind that individuals can vary greatly in terms of their respective comfort zones, values and boundaries. Furthermore, different cultures have different views on personal sharing in the workplace, and for some, maintaining hierarchical layers is rooted in respect and tradition, not simply beaurocracy.

Examples of struggles that leaders can share that lead to humanizing themselves and bonding with their team are:

- Not knowing what you wanted to do with your career or life
- Working for a toxic boss (remember: no names of people or organizations when you share)

- Getting passed up for a promotion
- Trying something new and failing
- Losing a key account
- Managing a project that fails
- Losing key team members
- Regretting not going for a great opportunity
- Not speaking up even though you had something valuable to contribute that would have made a difference
- Rejection (especially if you are a sales leader and coaching a sales team)
- Bouncing back after failure or rejection
- Realizing something wasn't for you (your startup business failed, or you switched careers after you hated your first career or became completely burned out)

Notice none of the above suggestions include sharing marital struggles, addiction, childhood abuse, or any other form of trauma. As a leader, your experience can be a vast library of teaching moments for your team, but you are still allowed to be a person who keeps their private life private.

If the aim is to create a safe space, leading with vulnerability, and sharing mistakes as a way of humanizing ourselves as leaders, goes a very long way. Put another way, rank, title, and a laundry list of career accomplishments can alienate a team from their leader, but we can all relate to adversity, failure, and setbacks.

The other critical aspect of creating a safe space is to ask questions, of both a business and personal nature, out of genuine curiosity. This step can't be faked, forced, or flipped through to get to the next step. Even if a leader does open up with vulnerability, sharing their ups and downs and mistakes, they are talking before they are listening.

Sharing your journey as a leader, scars and all, lands a whole lot better once you've learned a few things about your new team member. Examples of questions that can open dialogue at this early stage include;

    a. What made you decide to join ABC Co.?
    b. What led you to study engineering in school?
    c. What do you enjoy about the work you do?
    d. What do you do for fun outside of work?
    e. Where is your favorite place you've ever travelled to?

There are many other questions in context that can help open the conversation, such as asking about their relocation if your newest addition moved to accept the job. You might ask questions about their experience at college if they are a recent graduate or went to a storied university (or an alma mater you share in common). Sporting events, long weekends, or other current events are other great places to start.

Highly divisive topics, which can include political or religious conflicts, are typically dangerous places to begin as conversation starters. Remember, the goal is to create rapport. Even if you have strong beliefs in certain areas, those beliefs are best kept to yourself at this early stage. After all, it's a lot easier to accept a difference of opinion if it comes from someone you respect. Give your team members a chance to get there by building your working relationship intentionally and respectfully.

Take notes if you need to, because one of the best ways to damage trust early is to forget the important details your team shares with you; from whether or not they have kids (and their names and ages) to serious allergies, to favorite shows. How does it make you feel when someone at work asks, "how did your daughter Sara's team fare in their ringette tournament on the weekend?"

Remembering details that are important to others shows them that they are important to you, which is a third way you can show your team that your office is a safe space. If a leader can do that, they will have successfully gotten to the start line of possibly the greatest trek a leader is privileged enough to take – to walk alongside their team through their greatest triumphs and challenges as a trusted advisor and wise council.

Now that you've laid the foundation for a safe space for all of your team members, it's time to meet each of them where they are in their growth and development journeys.

Skill Two: *Meet your team where they are*

One challenge many leaders face is outpacing their team. That is, they give advice they know their team will need, but before the team can appreciate why they need it. At the heart of this discrepancy are two key concepts; importance and relevance. It is important for a parent to teach their child how to drive safely, obeying the rules of the road – however it is not relevant until they are a teenager. Similarly, it's important to make sure your team stays up to date on new technology, and new SOP's (standard operating procedures), however it's not relevant for a team member who is two months away from retirement.

It is important for leaders to know each team member's challenges and opportunities, as well as skills and motivation, well enough to offer specific and timely guidance. This customized, 'one size fits one' approach dictates that we get to know our team well enough to meet them where they are, even if you as a leader may have crossed the career milestone they are struggling with 20 years ago. There are only two ways to get there with each team member; intention, and time with. You have to care enough to want to learn about them, and you have to put in the time, meeting by meeting, and one water cooler conversation or coffee break at a time.

One helpful paradigm to understand 'where your team is at' is the Stages of Change Model, originally proposed by Dr.'s Prochaska and DiClemente in 1983[15] as part of smoking cessation research. It has since been more widely accepted as a useful model for understanding behavior change, which is exactly what we are intending to accomplish when we offer our team feedback (we'll come back to feedback in skill nine).

The five stages of the stages of change model are as follows;

1. Precontemplation (Not Ready)

People in the Precontemplation stage do not intend to take action in the foreseeable future, usually measured as the next six months. Being uninformed or under-informed about the consequences of one's behavior may cause a person to be in the Precontemplation stage. Multiple unsuccessful attempts at change can lead to demoralization about one's perceived ability to change. 'Precontemplators' are often characterized in other theories as resistant, unmotivated, or unready for help.

2. Contemplation (Getting Ready)

Contemplation is the stage in which people intend to change in the next six months. They are more aware of the pros of changing, but are also acutely aware of the cons. In a meta-analysis across 48 health risk behaviors, the pros and cons of changing were equal[16]. This weighting between the costs and benefits of changing can produce a stalemate of sorts that can cause people to remain in this stage for long periods of time. This phenomenon is often characterized as chronic contemplation or behavioral procrastination. Individuals in the Contemplation stage are not ready to be pushed into taking immediate action.

3. Preparation (Ready)

Preparation is the stage in which people intend to take action in the immediate future, usually measured as the next month. Typically, they have already taken some significant action in the past year. These individuals have a plan of action, such as joining a gym, seeking a mentor, talking to their physician, or relying on a DIY (do it yourself) approach.

4. Action

Action is the stage in which people have made specific overt modifications to their behaviors within the past six months. Because action is observable, the overall process of behavior change often has been equated with action.

5. Maintenance

Maintenance is the stage in which people have made specific overt modifications in their behaviors and are working to prevent relapse; however, they do not apply change processes as frequently as do people in the Action phase. While in the Maintenance stage, people are less tempted to relapse and grow increasingly more confident that they can continue their changes. Based on self-efficacy data, researchers have estimated that Maintenance lasts from six months to about five years[15].

It is worth mentioning that the stages of change model also includes a sixth stage; relapse[15]. While the mention of relapse brings up connotations of a smoker falling back into the habit, or a heavy drinker 'falling off the wagon', this is not why we are including it here. People can relapse in terms of their thinking, too.

You might have a direct report who falls into 'victim thinking', feeling like everything happens *to* them. They might complain about how (they perceive) 'everyone has it easier than them'.

Keeping in mind the disclaimer on scope of practice, you may have had coaching conversations with your direct report, and helped them shift their thinking from 'victim' to 'victor' where they are more resilient and able to see challenges as opportunities. That being said, a demotion, relationship break-up, or death of a loved one (in addition to countless other stressors) may send your direct report right back to 'victim' reactions and thoughts. Coaching, like exercise, or most other things in life, is not a straight line to success.

If you experience a direct report regressing or relapsing in their professional development, attitude, and growth, have faith. What's worked in the past is likely to work again. Keep in mind that more effective than any question or piece of advice you've likely given them – is your attention. Reserving judgement, creating a safe space, and meeting them where they are (as well as the skills you'll read about next) are most likely going to build them right back up should they seem to regress in their development from time to time.

Meeting your team where they are is an essential skill to creating alignment, one of the skill gaps leaders cited most often in our State of Leadership Readiness survey from chapter three. One of the best ways to understand where each team member is at any given moment, from a skill, attitude, and perspective standpoint, is to master the third coaching skill.

Skill Three: *Ask profound questions*

In order to open up better conversations with their teams, leaders must learn to ask more, and better questions. Recall Nicole Jansen's advice, "questions lead, and answers follow".

Questions almost always lead to better conversations than statements do. Statements 'tell' your team what to do, or what to think. Questions are an invitation to your team to co-create solutions to their challenges, and pathways to their goals.

Questions are also more effective than statements for another reason. Statements often bottleneck you as the leader. If you are always *telling* your team what to do, by default you must always *know* what to do. This slows the progress of the organization down to how available you can be to your team. Without you to tell them what to do (and often how to do it) how can they know they're on the right track? Asking questions avoids you becoming the bottleneck. As we like to say, it helps you become more of a boat engine, and less of a boat anchor, for your team.

Finally, asking questions of your team can lead to your team coming up with their own answers, and their own commitments. If you tell your team what to do, the best you can hope for is compliance – the team doing what you said. When your team *tells you* what they will do, they become *committed* – to their own their promises as now their integrity and reputation – their character – are on the line.

Below is a bullet point guide to asking better questions.

  a. Without patting yourself on your back or posturing, always think 'what is the smartest question I can ask right now?'
  b. Ask the same question as many different times as necessary if it hasn't been answered fully or deeply enough
  c. If necessary, ask questions that force a team member to change their perspective if they 'can't see the forest through the trees' (for example "what advice would you give your child or best friend if they were in your shoes?")

d. Ask questions that challenge your direct reports to come up with the answer(s) instead of always giving it to them. This will increase their commitment level and resulting action(s).

e. Per above, Stanford Graduate School of Business Instructor Ed Batista suggests spending more time asking questions out of inquiry to open conversations rather than rushing to find solution(s) too early[17]. The better leaders can do this, Batista suggests, the more likely an employee is to come up with their own solution[17].

f. There are few, if any, questions more profound than 'why?'. There are also few questions that place someone on the defensive faster. "Why does this truly matter to you?" can lead to a profound discussion on purpose. "Why did you do that?" leads your team to clam up and get defensive. Use 'why' wisely!

One particularly useful tool in the leaders' toolbox comes by combining *b* and *f* above; namely, the "5 why's" suggested in Jim Collins' bestselling book Good to Great[18]. In short, ask your direct report(s) why a particular outcome goal matters to them, or why they chose their profession. The "5 why's" then goes deeper, asking why again, in differing ways, to get to a deeper answer.

The story that comes to mind is working with a client who came so close to a breakthrough so many times in pursuing her fitness goals many years ago. As her fitness coach, I asked why we always seemed to progress in waves, or like a yo-yo, only to have a relapse. As we worked through some examples, this client revealed that they had moved 17 times by the time they were 19. Then it hit me like a ton of bricks. They weren't quitting because it was hard. They were distancing themselves as we became closer, because they were afraid to lose anyone close to them. Think about how many friends they had to say goodbye to during those tough formative years as they moved so often!

You can also ask why in many different ways. Why can be how. *How would your life be different or better if you achieve that goal?*

Why can be what. *What would it take for you to be fulfilled in your career? What is it about this line of work that is so important to you?* NCADV CEO Ruth Glenn gets her team to focus on the organizations' mission by asking her team *"what are we contributing to the world?"*

Why can be when. *When will you know that you have found the right role (or career or company) for yourself?*

One other example of a profound question is the defining success question. As a leader, or as a coach, you'll often be counted upon during times of change, crisis, chaos, or confusion. If you are to provide clarity, calm, and confidence in your team at such times, it's essential to create focus. A perfect question to achieve this when your team is confused, overwhelmed, or in need of guidance is, "what does success look like?"

By having your team define the 'goal posts', so to speak, you are now empowered to understand the central issue(s), how this is affecting your team, what success entails, and what might get in the way. It also helps clarify what support, resources, and coaching and direction your team might need. "What does success look like?" is different for everyone, which is why it's such an important question to ask at the onset of any complex challenge.

Besides including the above as examples, there is a reason we are not including a comprehensive list of profound questions.

'Profound' is relative to its context. A profound question ceases to be so if it is simply memorized and regurgitated by someone who is not wholly present to the person to whom they are asking said question.

The key to asking a profound question is to be wholly present to the other person. When we are fully present to others (skill five), we quiet our minds, and enter a more empathetic state. Have you ever noticed that you'll often yawn after someone else does? We are actually six times more likely to yawn after someone else does because of 'social mirroring'[19]. Humans are social creatures. When others open up to us, and we are fully present, doing our best listening, we gain access to a profound wisdom, well beyond logic or academic training. We can help others access their hidden wisdom in this state too!

The biggest secret to being wholly present lies in how we listen to those we are trying to coach. Time to turn our attention on how to become better listeners!

> **Concept to Application**
>
> I was working with a client recently who share that one of their team members made a mistake that really cost the company. The leader was getting berated by the angry customer, and made sure their team member was there to hear the impact of their actions. Afterwards they asked their direct report, "now do you know why [following the systems] is so important?"
>
> In our coaching we discussed the spectrum of high quality versus low quality questions. This leaders' strategy of having their team member hear the impact to the customer was a good one, however their question led to a 'yes' or 'no' answer, and most team members would default to yes for fear of losing their job.
>
> We went through a series of questions that might serve their purposes better here, with the end result being, "what did you learn from this experience?"
>
> My client liked that question, because it wasn't condescending, and it allowed him to meet their team where they were (skill two), and expose any learning gaps, rather than inviting a compliant 'yes'.

Skill Four: *Listening to understand*

If communication is like a coin, then the flip side of 'asking better questions' is doing better listening. I believe that listening can be thought of on a spectrum; from low to high quality. As Ed Batista puts it, hearing and listening are not the same thing. "Hearing is a cognitive process that happens internally — we absorb sound, interpret it, and understand it. But listening is a whole-body process that happens between two people that makes the other person truly feel heard."[17]

As described in our book "Life Literacy", my coauthors Matt Young, Nelson Soh and I argue there are three different levels of listening. The following excerpt is as explained in Life Literacy[20].

First, low-quality, or Level One, listening is "listening to respond." In many cases when a low-level listener hears something, they want to respond so badly they won't even let the other person finish speaking. They interrupt to say their part.

In other cases, the listener focuses on only one point the speaker has made, so that everything they say afterwards has been missed. In their impatience to reply to the point, or story that resonated with them, a low-level listener has responded to one piece but missed the story altogether. In our coaching business, low-level listening is downright hazardous. In many cases, the problem that a client leads with is not the problem at all but rather a symptom. A Level One listener would miss this, quickly jumping in and solving the wrong problem. Whereas a wise coach asks more questions and finds the root of the problem.

A Level Two listener is someone who listens to understand. This may manifest itself by asking clarifying questions, once the other person has finished speaking. "If I heard you correctly Donna, you don't feel appreciated at work and you wish someone would notice all of the extra effort you put in without being asked. Did I catch your meaning?"

It's important to note any skill can be taken too far, or used too frequently, thereby diminishing its value. If you were to ask a clarifying question after everything that your friend says, they would likely end the painful interaction rather quickly. Besides asking clarifying questions, the most noticeable difference between a Level One and a Level Two listener is their focus. Level One listeners frequently focus on themselves. They are listening to respond with their stories and sometimes even waiting to 'one-up' the speaker. A Level Two listener is focused on the speaker.

They are present and listening with their entire body, ensuring they grasp the speaker's meaning.

What is listening with your whole body? Well, research out of UCLA in 2009 concluded that communication is 55 percent body language, 38 percent paralanguage (pitch, volume, intonation, etc.) and only seven percent verbal[21]. Listeners are perceptive to what we communicate far beyond our spoken word, so speaking is a more complex skill than most of us realize. We could write an entire book on body language alone! But here it's important to at least mention how critical the alignment between our spoken word and physical stance becomes. You can tell your boss that you are listening but if you roll your eyes, or stare out the window, while they are speaking, you're giving a very different impression. Level Two listeners are present and in the moment when conversing with others. As you will see, this is also true for a Level Three listener.

The trademark of a Level Three listener is someone who listens not just to understand meaning, but also to understand how they may be of service. If Level One is listening to respond and Level Two is listening to understand, then Level Three is listening to add value. This is not always strategic value. Level Three listeners most often listen with empathy. This listener may be a strategist who can add business acumen and insight to an idea. Or just be one who listens with immense care and concern and an innate desire to see the other person succeed. This type of listener may make a helpful introduction, nominate a friend for an award, or speak to their boss suggesting that another person deserves a promotion.

To put it simply, a Level One listener listens with their mouth, a Level Two listener listens with their ears and brain, and a Level Three listener listens with their soul. I'm sure we've all felt the difference!

Many of the leaders we've coached over the years find it a useful 'litmus test' to ask themselves what level of listening they are practicing. You might decide to reflect on the conversation you just had, or you might look back at the end of a busy week and ask how you did. In any event, reflection and intention help us get better at anything we set our minds to.

If our intention is to listen at a higher level, there are several requisites to achieve our aim;

- A. Keen awareness and control of body language (maintaining eye contact, ensuring arms aren't crossed, and leaning slightly forward, for example).
- B. Not needing to talk, especially if a team member is thinking, taking time to respond, or even slightly emotional (though it is critical that leaders realize the limitations of their training, scope of practice, and comfort level in dealing with personal challenges that may arise. You are not supposed to be a trained psychologist, simply a novice coach).
- C. Fighting the first urge to respond- listen to the whole sentence, statement, issue, or challenge.
- D. Rephrasing what you've heard to ensure you got it right- ask!
- E. Avoiding distractions. In fact, staying present is a skill in and of itself, which we will dive into next.

What kind of listener do you think you are? Recall from the first chapter that leaders are running two parallel races; their own development and the development of their teams. Remember that self-awareness is the start line to your race, and that self-awareness requires self-reflection. Reflect on recent conversations you've had at work or at home. What percentage of the time do you think you are doing level three listening? Level two? Level one?

Nick Roud shares how effective listening helps leaders take better action and drive better results. "*An effective leader of today has the ability to listen to a whole heap of different types of music all at once (let's call that your data). As they listen in, they start to see themes, feel vibes, taste what is pure and what is just background stuff. They feel their gut and listen to what it's telling them.*

By listening and I mean really listening the effective leader can now focus on and act accordingly to what the real need of the organization is. They hone in on just a few specific things and nothing more than three or four highly focused points.

Effective Leaders of today (and tomorrow) will need to harness and strengthen their (senses) if they want to be a successful leader and an in-demand leader."

Keep in mind that no one is perfect, and that's not even a goal. The goal of personal and professional development is to be better than you were yesterday. Reflect, set your intentions (and make plans) to improve, and then do your best – that's all any of us can do!

When you release yourself from the pressure to be perfect, it allows you to be far more present in each conversation you'll have with your team. This is a key aspect of becoming a better coach, and it's where we will shift our attention to next. But first, a powerful lesson on just how important listening is as a leader, and how it can have a much bigger impact than many of us think.

Simone Campbell shared that her most pressing mission – that which she is most focused on accomplishing – is to improve "the capacity to listen to one another. The capacity to have a heart that's bigger than just my tribe." Campbell mentioned being a great storyteller as a common trait of great leaders, and she adds that "storytellers are nothing if they're not good listeners. They need the capacity to listen to acquire new stories".

What an amazing world we would live in if we could choose, like Simone Campbell, to think bigger than our tribe, or our agenda. To make life better for all, not just ourselves. To Sister Simone Campbell, listening is that powerful, and that transformative; it can make the whole world better.

> ### Concept to Application
>
> If you were to teach your team how to listen at level three, how would you do it? One of my coaching colleagues and I were facilitating a leadership retreat in Las Vegas for a group of 26 leaders in 2022. We explained the concept, and broke the team into pairs. We were all in one conference ballroom, and to challenge our group, we had them all stay in the same room. With thirteen different conversations happening at once, we turned the music up, and tasked the group with asking each other, "why is this more than a job for you?"
>
> By making the assignment personal, and by adding distractions, we forced our clients to focus more on what- rather – *who*- was in front of them at that moment. After the exercise, they all had the same feedback: they couldn't hear anything else except the person they were paired with.
>
> In September of 2023, I was speaking at a human resources conference in Edmonton, Alberta. We tried the same exercise, but this time with 125 people – it became a dull roar! Participants shared that while the level of noise was distracting at first, it forced them to concentrate deeper on their partner (in this case, asking them what their purpose was). Participants even shared they experienced questioning their own purpose, and building upon it, based on the depth of conversations they had – at deafening volume – with in some cases perfect strangers. Level three listening at its best!

Skill Five: *Be present*

One of the best ways to become a better listener is to become a better participant in the conversation, and of the meeting itself. My mentor Matt Young calls this the '100% rule'; be 100% present wherever you are. Don't think about a looming deadline while you're in a one on one with a direct report, and don't be thinking about the weekend at 3:45pm on a Thursday. Conversely, be present for conversations with family, while playing with your kids, or while socializing with friends.

Be present. If you're thinking about work while you're with family, they know it. If you're thinking about the weekend while you're at work, chances are you're less productive. You may now even have to work on the weekend because you didn't take advantage of the focused task time you had during the week. Be present.

Recall the landmark study out of UCLA in 2009, 55% of all communication is conveyed via our body language, 38% through our paralanguage, and only 7% through the words we use[21]. This means that over 90% of what others hear has nothing to do with the words coming out of our mouths. People are smart – they can tell if you're not engaged or not listening, regardless of what you say. Even if you do 'say the right things', your words will have all the more impact if you are more present since 93% of communication is non-verbal[21].

Lastly, it's very hard to ask profound questions (skill three) if we aren't curious about the person we are speaking with. It's very hard to be curious if you aren't present. Instead of asking great questions, you could be thinking about your next meeting, or a looming deadline. By clearing your mind of everything that happened before this meeting, and refusing to focus on everything after – you become very present. Sometimes, even if we don't have any profound questions or great advice to offer, simply being present is enough. A lot of people don't have a mastermind group, executive coach, or mentor to turn to with their challenges. Being there for your team gives them an outlet they might not have anywhere else in their lives. It's not always appropriate to turn to your friends, significant other, or coworkers with your challenges. Being present adds value to your team, period.

These coaching skills also build on each other, so being present also enables you to be a more effective coach by positioning your conversation and your relationship to be able to deliver on the other skills you'll read about through the rest of this chapter.

Being present also means focusing on your team more than your agenda. No matter how prepared you are for a meeting, the possibility always exists that the greatest value generated in the meeting happens in the spur of the moment. You might prepare for a coaching conversation with your direct report, with specific, meaningful feedback prepared in advance. You could walk in and deliver your great feedback, or – you could create a safe space, ask profound questions, listen to understand, and be present to the pace and direction the conversation naturally travels. Maybe it steers right back to the feedback you've prepared, but maybe a deeper, more meaningful conversation opens up. Only by being present can you detect that a more valuable conversation must be had than the one you prepared for.

Ultimately, being present means focusing on the conversation – the process – not just the outcome. It means being prepared enough that you're not preoccupied, but also present enough that you're not just listening to reply or present your agenda (don't forget skill four!)

Preparation involves reviewing your notes beforehand and visualizing what your team might need from you, or what they might need help with the most. True presence means eliminating all distractions so that you can be completely engaged with the person in front of you. The more prepared you are, the easier it is to be present. The more present you are, the easier it is to understand what strategic outcomes need to flow from your conversation.

Before we jump ahead to outcomes however, a great coach focuses on alignment, which will be the focus of the next two coaching skills.

Skill Six: *Uncover their values and currency*

If you haven't already learned this – make a point to remember that listening leads to learning. Often as leaders we get caught in the trap of downloading. We download marching orders, tasks, strategies, deliverables, and reminders. We do need to communicate deliverables and keep the bus rolling as leaders, but remember that we're not learning when we're 'downloading'.

Listening is akin to uploading. In keeping with this analogy, the more time we spend listening to our team, the better 'software' we upload to allow us to work effectively with our team as a unit, and with each member individually. We learn more about them which helps us work better together.

Among the most important pieces of software for us to upload from our teams are their core values and their currency. My book series "Success is a System" goes into depth on core values, and features several exercises on how to uncover one's values. Three such examples are 'always/ never statements', how you spend your money, and what you'd choose to pass down.

Always/ never statements are good clues to uncovering your values. Simply complete the sentences "I always

_____" and "I never _____". Someone who always tips 20%, regardless of the quality of service received, might have a value of appreciation, or gratitude. A CFO who is always home for dinner might have a value of 'family' or 'balance'. Someone who is never late for meetings might have a core value of respect. They respect other people's time.

We all work hard for our money. As such, how we choose to spend our hard-earned paycheck says a lot about what we value. When I was building my coaching practice, the most responsible thing I could have done as an entrepreneur would have been preserve cash flow to extend the 'runway' of my business. Instead, I spent over $50,000 in the first five years on continuing education, and personal and professional growth. While proper education and training is important to any endeavor, I certainly could have spent less. While logic and reason called for saving, my number one core value is personal growth. This is not to say that our core values lead us to make poor financial decisions. Instead, our core values have a strong compelling pull on us in many situations, and trends in how we spend our money can offer clues as to our values. In other words, my decision didn't make sense from a financial point of view. It did make sense however, to anyone who knew my values.

In terms of what we'd choose to pass down, imagine you became suddenly ill, and you were having the last conversation you'd ever have with a loved one. In addition to telling them you loved them, what behaviors or values would you encourage them to live the rest of their lives honoring? What moral code would you hope they adopt? (I know, some of these exercises can get heavy – if you'd rather not think of an end-of-life scenario, pretend you're retiring on the beach, and won't see them as often, or training your replacement to lead your team – the spirit of the exercise is the same).

While our values act as our moral code, our currency is our motivational code. Let's say you have three children. If they are all refusing to go to bed, would you discipline them all the same? Chances are, a parent might threaten them with different consequences, or reward them with different methods. One child might respond to a point system ("you'll get a sticker if you go to bed on time" and 10 stickers might equal a new toy). One child might not respond until something they value is taken away ("go to bed or I'm taking away your favorite toy" – or phone for an older child). A third sibling might not choose to go to bed unless they get told a bedtime story (or three), or get to read 10 pages on their own.

In each of these cases, what resonates with someone enough to take action is their currency. I played football because I loved competition, especially the contact nature of football. I hated losing, even more than I liked winning. My son Chase played hockey for the social aspect – winning and losing barely even registered for him. My wife Maria is a twin. She's even more competitive than I am, especially with her twin sister Effie. We even have a family trophy that goes back and forth to the winning household of whatever games we come up with during that family get together.

People are complex, and multi-faceted. This means, they likely have more than one 'currency', and it is often contextual – changing with changing circumstances. A safety professional might spend their entire day finding ways to mitigate risk at work, then go on holidays a week later and try skydiving for a sense of adventure!

Sister Simone Campbell points out that many leaders tend to over-rely on structure. "Often leaders get mistaken as the folks who can create the structure. They set up elaborate structures, checklists, org charts and all that. That's not leadership; that's organization, and what gets missed is the energy – the power –

of a mission and vision. Too often in the complexity of corporate structure, the org chart dominates as opposed to the sense of shared mission."

People can be motivated by a great number of factors, and they'll rarely come up and tell you, "Nice to meet you boss – my name is George and my currency is people working in harmony". Instead, coaches need to rely on their repertoire of great skills, like asking profound questions (skill three), and listening to understand (skill four).

There's a powerful contrast in currency and output I've shared countless times with our team and clients over the years.

> *If you rule with an iron fist and command your team to be at their desk by eight, and stay there until five, you will achieve compliance. Your team will work just hard enough not to get fired. When instead leaders focus on appealing to the hearts and minds of their team, we can unlock their discretionary effort. Our team starts to bring their passion, creativity, and best ideas forward to solve problems and create magic rather than watching the clock.*

Uncovering your team's values and currency will be absolutely essential to effectively grasping skill ten, so make sure you are putting these skills into practice rather than speed-reading this book cover to cover!

Skill Seven: *Identify, amplify, and address*

Einstein famously said, "Everyone is a genius. But if you judge a fish by its ability to climb a tree, it will live its whole life believing that it is stupid."

When it comes to bringing out the best in their team, a coach must at some point learn the basics of talent development. In no way does this mean you must become an expert in talent identification, or that others' livelihoods are now completely in your hands. Ultimately, it comes down to observation, and then knowing what to do with what you see.

Because she sees the strengths in people, executive coach Nicole Jansen sometimes overlooks their weaknesses and shortcomings. To Jansen, you have to focus on the strengths, but you must also be aware of the weaknesses. Furthermore, Jansen explains that any strength taken to an extreme becomes a weakness. She advises leaders to see the greatness of others, but also be aware of who they are choosing to be in the moment.

> Note: There are many tools at the coaches' disposal when it comes to strengths and gaps. Check out different versions of a 360° review, and for strengths- based appraisals, check www.corestrengths.com or www.gallup.com

Observation, much like skill two (meeting your team where they are) often comes down to simply spending 'time with'. Add skills three (asking profound questions), four (listening to understand) and five (be present), and it becomes hard *not to* learn a lot about your team!

Beyond third-party professional assessments, there is also the performance review. Many companies now include a personal reflection and performance assessment. With observation, assessment, and open dialogue, every leader should become aware of every one of their team members' strengths in the short term. In the intermediate term, even the teams' 'blind spots' (surprise weaknesses or gaps) should become apparent.

As you've probably already guessed, finding out what your team's strengths and opportunities are is only part of the skill. The second piece is knowing what to do with that information. In his book, The Intelligent Leader, my friend and five-time Global Guru's executive coach of the year John Mattone calls this, "leveraging your gifts and addressing your gaps"[22]. One reason I'm an advocate for the Core Strengths™ set of assessments, is the focus on the linkage between strengths and values. While an NFL wide receiver might be born with 'great hands', most of us develop our strengths as a sequence of hundreds, if not thousands of choices. In other words, most of us choose our strengths more so than just being born with them.

According to Tim Scudder, *"strengths that are intentionally connected to core motives, by way of authentic reasons, tend to be most effective and sustainable in working relationships*[23]*"*. The last chapter dove into uncovering values and currency. When you know your teams' values and currency (core motives, to Scudder), you can understand *why* their strengths are what they are, and aren't. In short, you know why your team chooses their behaviors.

Think of a behavior, or social strength, as a tool, no different than a carpenter's hammer, screwdriver, or saw. Which tool is better; the hammer, screwdriver, or saw? That would depend on the job, wouldn't it? In coaching we often say, 'a hammer makes a terrible screwdriver', which means our behavioral strategy – the strength we bring to the table – must depend on the situation.

It's also important to understand that all strengths are valuable and important. While different situations can affect which strengths are more appropriate to call upon, so can different personality combinations, and the overall organizational culture.

A highly competitive former athlete might be a better fit for an ambitious athletic brand like Nike, than a company whose success is predicated upon collaboration, like a project management firm. This is not a rule, nor necessarily even a suggestion. We are merely painting a picture of connecting values, strengths, and ultimately – performance and sustainable success.

While anecdotal, our extensive experience is that people (and through them – organizations) see far greater return on investment (ROI) by 'doubling down' on strengths than they do spending too much time trying to shore up their weaknesses. Spending an equal amount of time developing strengths and weaknesses is a recipe for marginality.

In his book "Outliers", Malcolm Gladwell discusses the '10,000-hour rule', citing this as the amount of time required to achieve mastery in any given discipline[24]. What many people forget about Gladwell's 10,000-hour rule is the notion of 'intentional practice'; it's not the time itself, it's the choice to spend that much time getting better at what you love[24]. Bringing Gladwell's work back to ROI, you could spend 10,000 hours coaching and potentially become a world-class coach (if that is your passion), or spend 10,000 hours studying financial statements and likely become an incompetent accountant (if this is not your passion).

While you as the leader and coach of your team do need to point out and help your team address their performance shortfalls, it's also important that their functional role does not require high levels of competence in an area addressed as one of their weaknesses. This is talent development 101 – place your team members where they can contribute (and therefore receive) the most value.

Lastly, just as you did for yourself, remember to take attitude into account. My high school coach Joe Stambene tried to preach the importance of sound fundamentals, but always told his team, *'when you do make a mistake, do it going full speed'*. In other words, when your team commits a blunder while trying their hardest, commend them for their effort and tease out the learning moments. When your team isn't trying, that's when you have problems. One early warning sign of a 'checked out employee', is when they stop trying to learn, work on their mistakes, or get better at their existing strengths.

The great news as it relates to talent development for leaders coaching their teams is that you don't have to be better than your team to coach them. To help a team member continue to improve, you needn't have all the answers, just the questions. Instead of 'try this' or 'do that', consider, 'what do you need from me to reach or your goal?' or 'what obstacles do you need me to help remove in order for you to reach your target?'

Leveraging their strengths and managing their gaps is all about making forward progress. It's not always where the ship is at this moment that matters the most. It's often just as, if not more important, to focus on where the ship is headed.

With that, we turn to making sure your team knows where they're supposed to be headed.

Skill Eight: *Clarify expectations*

Have you ever been disappointed, or even downright mad, at a co-worker because they let you down? Have you ever been disappointed, and felt let down, even though you didn't spell out exactly what you were expecting from your co-worker? The root of a great many relationship breakdowns is a failure to live up to expectations, even if they were never expressed.

The more well-defined the destination (goal), the clearer the pathway (strategy or plan) becomes. No one likes to hit an ambiguous, moving target. This can actually be a source of disengagement, even stress, for your team. Few things can erode your team's engagement faster than seeing their hard work go to waste as the 'goal posts' change mid-project.

Success so often comes down to understanding the goal - understanding what a successful outcome looks like. Far too often in the world of work, team members walk away from a meeting assuming they know what's expected of them. Leaders assume the team knows what they need to do, who's doing it, and by when. Teammates assume that everyone who must contribute to a complex task will do their part and miraculously coalesce at the perfect time. One thing great project managers – great *leaders* – can do is to make sure everyone is clear on the target, the timeline, and the task owner(s) before strategy meetings are adjourned. An old cliché in the world of project management goes, 'well begun is half done'!

In our coaching practice, one of the most critical steps early on is defining each individual (or teams') scoreboard for success. That is, not everyone is motivated by increased revenues and profits, or career advancement. The role of the coach is to uncover what motivates their team (or each individual) and align this motivation to the work that must be done. Taking this notion one step further, great coaches align what matters to the individual with what matters to the organization. In other words, identifying how individual success leads to team success and how a team win helps each individual. This is how we move beyond cliches and truly get everyone on the team rowing in the same direction.

Great leader coaches set (or have the team member set) crystal clear deliverables, and then identify the obstacles in the way, and the resources (time, people, capital, skill development) required to accomplish the mission.

Questions you as the leader can ask before setting the team to task are;

   i. What do they understand their deliverable(s) to be?
   j. What resources do they need to achieve the mission? This could include budget, training, software, equipment, and logistical needs (like a Smartboard or meeting rooms booked, or marketing collateral printed for the big presentation).
   k. Who do they need support from to achieve the mission? Try to help your team zero in on exactly what and who they need, based on specific skills, experience, or perspective. Don't forget to include reporting relationships (who else they'll need approvals from).
   l. What support do they need from you as their leader?

Asking clarifying questions and setting clear expectations in advance helps you as the leader avoid becoming a micromanager. Instead, you can become seen as a great coach with impeccable follow up skills. Which kind of leader would you rather have? Which kind of leader would you rather *be*?

Finally, never take for granted how preparation time up front saves everyone time cleaning up messes on the back end.

Abraham Lincoln said it best, "Give me six hours to chop down a tree, and I will spend the first four sharpening the axe."

Clarifying expectations will save you, and your team a lot of headaches. That being said, nobody's perfect, and your team will miss the mark from time to time (so will you)! When this inevitability occurs, leaders need to master our next skill, the art of delivering feedback skillfully.

Skill Nine: *The art of feedback*

Feedback, at its finest, is an art more than a mere conversation. At its core, feedback is one of the most important tools of the trade for coaches. Feedback can help those in a leaders' care gain greater awareness, skills, and insight to greater performance. Well-delivered feedback can even help others realize their career objectives, if not dreams. That being said, feedback can also make recipients uncomfortable, especially when receiving 'constructive feedback'. Poorly delivered feedback can be the stuff of nightmares that leads would-be successes to leave not just their job – but their entire industry- before they realize their potential.

It is these nightmare scenarios, or a lack of enough constructive criticism growing up, that can make people uncomfortable with feedback that is anything other than 'great job Beth'. Leaders must remember that it takes a lot of care to hold others accountable – it would be easier not to have the conversation, but it would also be a grave disservice to your team.

Rachael Bosch, CEO of the feedback platform Candorly, shared with me over email four other reasons that feedback (on a larger scale) can be challenging;

1. It can be hard to select the right questions to get the data you need
2. Following up with your team or customers (depending on the type of survey) is often a manual process
3. The analysis of the data is also often a manual process, which opens the possibility of human error as well as the subjective nature of data interpretation
4. Systemized reports are "non-existent at worst, and ugly at best" in her words.

To help your team be more receptive to feedback, it's essential as a leader coach that your feedback is always delivered from a motivation to help. We must avoid the temptation to judge. Judgement is akin to condemnation, whereas feedback is akin to coaching. One way leader coaches can ensure they are delivering feedback, not judgement is to check the emotional root of their advice. Judgement usually comes from a kneejerk reaction, based on emotions of frustration, impatience, anger, or disappointment. Helpful feedback, especially when delivering potentially tough feedback, always comes from a place of care, trust, or even love.

When we focus on what matters (helping others get better) we are open to different ways of delivering our message. Great coaches combine care with curiosity. They care enough about their team to tackle difficult conversations head on, but they are patient enough to get there in whatever way works for their team, instead of sticking to their own preferred delivery method. Curiosity can be a superpower here as leader coaches stay present and apply different lines of questioning until they find a method or conversational approach that works.

Once we've learned to center ourselves as coaches, and improve the source of our feedback (our intent), it's time to learn how to improve the content of our feedback. There are three main types of feedback a leader can give, but only two they ever should.

1. Positive reinforcement: specific, meaningful praise (not just 'good job') timed as a team member 'connects the dots' or sees any other breakthrough. When offered in this way, feedback can galvanize learning and increase motivation to continue progressing in their role. Specific praise can and should also be given to team members who are going over and above, or who sacrifice for the betterment of the team. "Catch them doing right" as the saying goes. An example of positive feedback would be "I can tell how much preparation you put into your presentation today Cindy – you spoke eloquently, you seemed rehearsed yet conversational, and you did a great job on engaging the board members – well done!"
2. Constructive criticism: is feedback geared towards helping team members see better results. This may include pointing out blind spots, challenging limiting views or negative attitudes, questionable strategy, or less than acceptable execution. As noted above, even if the feedback stings at first, it is for the team members' benefit, and must be given with care, even if delivered firmly. One example of tough-but-fair constructive criticism would be, "Ted, I'll be candid – I'm a little disappointed in your market research. I know what you're capable of, and this isn't it. I specifically wanted you on this project because there was no room for error. What happened?"
3. Negative feedback: there is no room for this type of feedback in the coaches' repertoire. Negative feedback is usually rude, insulting, if not attacking. Examples of negative feedback include, "that was awful – what were you thinking?" or "you did a terrible job" or "did you try and mess this up?". Besides tone, the major difference

between constructive and negative feedback is that constructive feedback offers advice or strategies for improvement, if not at least recognition that the individual is capable of more. Constructive criticism can also be an invitation to find a solution together. Negative feedback is typically harsh criticism – judgement with no solution, or offer to help.

When we start with the right focus, and the right source (our intent), and then improve the nature (content), we come close to mastering our feedback delivery. Mastering the delivery of feedback has at least four distinct benefits;

a. Well-timed positive reinforcement can lead to an increase in the behaviors you want to see more of.
b. Differentiating constructive criticism from negative feedback can make those resistant to receiving feedback more coachable as they feel like it is less of an attack. They become more likely to see your intent to help, which makes them less defensive and more receptive to your message.
c. A team willing to be coached can 'course correct' faster, meaning performance can be improved in closer to real time.
d. A team comfortable with feedback will give each other feedback. This is called 'lateral accountability', and it is a cornerstone of a high performing team. In most organizations, too many things are happening too quickly, in too many places, for the feedback to always come from the boss. A great team holds each other accountable.

As leaders we can help our teams become more coachable and more open to feedback by helping them become more open to receiving it. Before we do that, it's imperative as leaders that we remain open to feedback. Two common 'feedback blocks' we see in coaching are, A) the inability for driven leaders to accept praise, and B) avoidance of constructive criticism from those who may have received too much negative, or even toxic feedback, in their past. NCADV CEO Ruth Glenn reminds us that "sometimes you have to hear the hard stuff rather than hide from it".

To enable the most driven leaders to accept more praise, we have two tips. First, ask yourself what kind of example you are setting – do you want your team to model your behavior; that it's all about the chase, and never about enjoying the journey? By being present, and letting praise sink in, you will feel greater appreciation for the work (and for your team), which is a healthier behavior to model than the kind of martyrdom many leaders exhibit.

Second, it's very hard to 'go the distance' – to make it far in business or in life, if we don't have balance. Celebrating the wins while driving for the next one is a healthier approach than constantly remaining in the hunt.

In order to help leaders change their perspective on constructive criticism, we offer several important lessons (or reminders).

1. Keeping focus in mind, make sure you as the leader are focused on the feedback (coaching) your team needs, not how you feel about feedback. Consider the other persons' feelings as you deliver feedback, but don't project your own views on feedback to your team.
2. It takes more care to give constructive criticism than it does to stay silent. If you don't care about someone, you can justify watching them struggle needlessly, or work harder than they need to, while achieving less than the desired result(s). If we care enough about that person,

we set our ego and our feelings aside, and give them the coaching they need.
3. If we avoid difficult conversations because it makes us uncomfortable, we 'pass on our baggage' to our team(s). Our hang-ups become theirs. This is also advice we give parents. If your child is told they are perfect just the way they are, instead of being told when their behavior is unacceptable, that child will go on to develop a very entitled and disillusioned self-concept and world view. If world-class athletes, famous actors, politicians and business leaders are expected to remain humble, then we need to teach this along the way. Being reminded (kindly and professionally) that we aren't perfect helps us to keep improving, and keeps us humble. Never forget as a leader that while it might involve an awkward conversation or two, feedback helps make your team better – and that is your job.

By demonstrating to our team(s) that we are open to feedback, we are modeling the behaviors we want to see in the world. That is great leadership by example. When your team sees you open to feedback, they have less justification to not be open to it themselves. Besides being a great example, two key reminders to teach your team to help them become more open to feedback are as follows;

1. Assume positive intent. As coaches we are huge believers in 'what we focus on grows'. If you are focused on the feedback you are receiving (or expect to receive) as being a form of judgement or condemnation, you're far more likely to frame the context or subtext of the feedback as a personal attack. If we assume that the person who is giving us feedback is doing so because they care, and

they're trying to help us – we are far more likely to accept it as a gift.

2. Ask 'where's the gift?'. As Ken Blanchard says, "feedback is the breakfast of champions"[25]. By harnessing the power of our subconscious mind to find actionable tidbits we can use to grow as professionals and as leaders, feedback becomes like a free book. Essentially, unless someone is giving us negative feedback (which can be a personal attack), they are offering us free advice on how we can improve. By asking 'where's the gift?', we are adopting a hungry 'student of the game' mentality which helps us to keep growing and getting better. Sister Simone Campbell jokes that feedback is a gift – "even if we don't want it".

The next three points on feedback involve focus, frequency and timing. As far as focus goes, always keep the focus on your team, not you. Your team does not want to hear "here's what I did" or even "here's what I would do". Similarly, it can be dangerous to tell your team "here's what you should do" (and telling people what to do is *not* coaching). Your job as their leader is not to be smarter, or have all of the answers all of the time. Your job is to help them be better at their jobs.

In terms of feedback frequency, for the most part, the more often the better, so long as your team isn't tuning you out like a broken record. One way to avoid this is to vary how you deliver your message. Saying the same thing 100 times over is painful for all parties involved. Finding 100 different ways to say the same thing until your message gets through is great communication, and patient leadership. Let common sense and curiosity be your guides.

In terms of timing, again common sense is your best bet. There are four key instances worth mentioning;

i. The 24-hour rule. You don't always need to take 24 hours, but avoid giving feedback when you are angry, or reacting emotionally. Remember to start with the best source and be centered on the right motivation and emotions.

ii. Respect their boundaries. It's important to remember that roles, titles, and reporting structure can create a power differential. Your direct reports may feel that they need to 'do right by you' in order to be considered for promotion or advancement opportunities. As a leader we can't make assumptions about our team's boundaries, work ethic, or life balance being similar to our own. Engage in open dialogue on your expectations on reply turnaround times if you're going to be sending your team emails, text messages, or calls outside of normal working hours.

iii. Performance reviews. As their leader coach, your team should receive lots of feedback from you in near real time. Their performance review should be the summation of the feedback trends received over the year. As a golden rule, no new feedback should be introduced during their performance review.

iv. Address it when you see it. Bestselling author and Founder of Level Five Selling John Hoskins, in his podcast "Coaching the Coach", says the best time to deliver feedback is "when the sweat is still on the brow".

Our final feedback tip, and one of our most important, is all about care. Keeping in mind that the focus of feedback is to be on your team – not you. This means accepting two inevitabilities. First, as a leader you cannot let your relationship with feedback impair your ability to give feedback to your team. If you struggle when others hold you accountable, you're likely to shirk away from having these conversations with your team. This means you are not doing your job as a leader. Your job is to bring out the best in your team, and you can't do that if you don't share with them what they need to improve. Second, it takes a lot of care to have difficult conversations.

Throughout our careers, we have had to have a lot of challenging conversations, and even for experienced coaches, it can make us uncomfortable. One thing we have advised leaders and other coaches on over the years is that it's always easier to avoid the difficult conversation. However, this means you are choosing your comfort over your team's growth. No leader worth following would be okay with that choice, and we know you're not either.

Skill Ten: *Align personal and organizational objectives*

As mentioned throughout this book, the skills of a great coach multiply when used in conjunction. You might not apply all of the skills described herein at once, but great coaches often use varying combinations of these skills at any given time, especially when they are at their best. Keeping this in mind, if you've created a safe space (skill one), met your team where they're at (skill two), asked profound questions (skill three), listened to understand (four), remained present (five), uncovered their values and currency (six), clarified expectations (eight), and given feedback skillfully (nine), then you have achieved several key outcomes;

- Built a solid rapport and a foundation of trust with your team
- Gotten to know your team on a deeper level

- Started to understand their motivation; their currency
- Helped them to understand their role, and why it matters (central to skill seven)
- Moved your team beyond compliance (doing the minimum) to a place of commitment (doing what is required)

With this foundation in place, we can begin to create win-win scenarios, by applying our understanding of their motives and values, and creating intersections with job duties and the overarching organizational plan. The key here is alignment, not manipulation. This is not an exercise in dangling a carrot ("if you do X for me, I'll do Y for you"). Rather, it's an opportunity to add purpose and meaning into the team's work ("if we can achieve X, here's how it benefits you personally", or "here is what the company is trying to accomplish, and where we need your skill set and experience").

Continuing the building block methodology of how all of these skills work together, if we can align personal motive to organizational objective, we create commitment (discretionary effort) to the cause, rather than compliance (doing the perceived minimum to avoid negative consequences). There are several ways a skilled coach can accomplish this with their team(s);

1. Leveraging strengths (skill seven). "Damon, we're going to need your keen eye for detail if we're going to wow our new biggest client. Suzy, we need your project management leadership to keep everyone on task and on time. Farrah, we need your creative genius to create the best marketing assets we ever have!"
2. Build a vision of a better tomorrow. The team is likely already bought into the organizational vision – 'being number one' or 'creating a carbon neutral future'. Here

we mean a better future for themselves. I remember being inspired by the story of one founder who had a team of 40 employees, and did not want to lay any of them off during a recession. He met with the team, and laid out the harsh reality the company was facing. Collectively, the team decided everyone in the company would take a pay cut so that no one had to lose their job. With a full team, they were able to come out of the recession faster than companies who made deep staffing cuts. As soon as the company was in a better financial position, all those who stayed through the tough times received raises to bring them back to where they were, plus a little extra to say thanks!

3. Sell the experience. Not everyone on your team will be with you for their entire career, and that is not a bad thing. Just because you know Dave from human resources is leaving at the end of the year doesn't mean you need to start creating distance. As long as Dave doesn't become a toxic influence on the rest of the team, he can still play a very valuable role. Point out learning experiences (or getting the experience to teach more junior employees) that will serve Dave well in his new position. As leaders, we must never forget to remind our teams that every experience shapes them, and every bit of experience makes them more valuable to the team. Even the ability to hire for a different department might be an experience Dave would appreciate before he moves on to his next company. Of course, this works even better for team members interested in building a career, whether with your company or not. When you as a leader turn every 'job' into an opportunity, you become a highly effective leader, and a pretty decent coach!

4. Building opportunity out of scarcity. Sometimes there are jobs that need doing that no one really wants to do. It might be changing light bulbs, plunging toilets, taking inventory, or any number of less popular tasks. It's usually easy to find someone willing to give the big presentation, or fly to New York to pitch the firm's biggest client. Sometimes your longer-term thinkers can find motivation in less desirable tasks by reminding them that leaders need to step up and take full responsibility for a job well done. The higher the career aspirations, the more things that will inevitably fall on your team's plate that aren't necessarily in their job description. If they want to own their own business, or to become the CEO one day, they need to learn now what accountability and 'stepping up' are all about.

5. Leadership by example. Perhaps you've just promoted Gina, and she informs you she's feeling a bit of new leader 'imposter's syndrome'. As Gina's coach, you could ask her questions (don't forget skill three) about her team, and what work is – and isn't – getting done. By temporarily taking on some of the tasks that don't have an owner, Gina could be sending a strong 'leadership by example' message to her team. If they see her step up, and then she asks them to do the same, they don't have a lot of excuses for why they won't answer the call!

Aligning values and mission to decision-making also allows leaders to make the right strategic and character decisions at the organizational level. Ruth Glenn shares the story of connecting with a wealthy individual who was donating a lot to the NCADV, but was making a list of demands and made the team feel like they were drifting away from the mission. It ended in a "very, very nasty break up". Lawyers had to get involved, and Ruth felt like this story reinforced what leadership is to her. "Integrity and ethical leadership; if it doesn't feel quite right it's important to pay attention to those instincts and check in with the team". They all felt in this instance that they should break off the relationship. "Make sure you live to your mission, even in the most uncomfortable of times".

Values also have a lot to do with conflict. According to Core Strengths™ theory, we only go into conflict when something we value is threatened[23]. Starting with ourselves, we can start to bring ourselves out of conflict when we shift our energy from trying to win an argument to becoming curious about what is triggering us. You might ask yourself 'which of my values is being compromised or threatened right now?'

When we can do this for ourselves, we can start to help mitigate conflict among our teams by asking the right questions, and trying to understand what each of our team members needs in the moment, and why they are being triggered. Recall from chapter three that conflict resolution was the biggest skill gap reported by the leaders we surveyed. Knowing your values and the values of your team gives you an upper hand as a leader when it comes to navigating conflict.

For Sister Simone Campbell, alignment is about building bridges. "I've come to realize that bridges get built not with the extremes, but with pillars that are closer together to lessen the spans. It's about creating conversation that creates understanding." To Campbell, "discovery and understanding new insights delights my heart."

In summary, when you've put in the time, and applied sound coaching fundamentals along the way, you have built a very solid foundation with your team. Upon that foundation of rapport and trust, it is the job of every leader to galvanize the commitment of their team towards organizational objectives. As Dr. Marilyn

Taylor puts it, "We must make better decisions by focusing on what matters instead of what distracts us and demands our attention".

Our next two skills are about realizing multiple strategic possibilities, and then helping translate the teams' commitment into decisive action. Whether we are building people up or building companies, all of our results live on the other side of *action*!

Skill Eleven: *See multiple possibilities*

Our results in any endeavor depend on the action we take. As a simple rule, the quality and quantity of action we take dictates the quality of results we can expect. The catch here, is that we can't take an action we can't see. Put another way, we can't launch a strategy or implement an idea we don't think of.

Part of a coach's job is to understand where your team is headed, and then help them see multiple pathways to get there. What most of us see as possibilities is tied directly to what we believe to be possible, and have the knowledge and experience to envision. A writer who has never worked in digital marketing might not think of deploying tools like HootSuite that allow users to enter their post, and schedule it to go live across multiple platforms. An experienced social media copywriter or digital marketer, however, knows how to triple their productivity in this example because of their knowledge and experience.

As a coaching book, we won't be diving into tech stacks or productivity tools – though they do exist, and are worth examining, or asking your more tech-savvy colleagues who have probably already done their research!

Where we will spend our time together to be able to see – and seize – new opportunities – is on our focus and our beliefs.

Focus is the easier concept to grasp for leaders. Try this exercise next time you are walking down a busy hallway or downtown sidewalk. What color are most of the outfits? You might say black or brown – common colors, especially in today's business attire. Now – look again but focus on a color, say blue or red. No doubt, you start seeing a lot more of that color. Anyone who recently purchased a new car can tell you the same thing. They never noticed how many Toyota 4Runner's there are on the roads until they bought one.

When we shift our focus, we change what we see. This could be red outfits among the predominantly neutral colors, or Toyota SUV's among the sea of vehicles in any major city. More impactfully, it can be whether we choose to focus on problems, or on opportunities. This is not to suggest that you ignore problems, of course not. You need to pay your bills, and respond to challenges at home, and you need to 'put out fires' from time to time at work. The theme here is focus. No doubt you've worked with others who always see the one cloud in the sky, or complain about how much tax they'll have to pay after a raise. Pessimists see a problem with every solution.

You've probably also worked with, or went to school with, someone you pegged as a genius. Did you peg them as a genius because they have an IQ above 160 (genius level)? Chances are you don't know their IQ test scores; you're just blown away by how their mind works. You might conclude, "whoever invented the Internet is a genius"

'Genius', in this application, is not measured by IQ. It's experienced as an exception to the norm. 'How did she solve the Rubik's Cube®?', or 'How did they solve today's Wordle in two tries?!'

In these instances, the people we experience as 'geniuses' focus where (or on what) the rest of us don't. Warren Buffett focuses on how stock market fluctuations can create good investment opportunities, while so many others focus on that red line going down, fearing that their investment is going to be worthless soon.

For Nina Bouzamondo-Bernstein, her focus has helped her become remarkably resourceful. The young founder advises her network, often students, "what are your resources? What do you have access to? Be willing to put in the work to find the resources to make your life easier. Go online and find a free PDF version of the course textbook, or skip breakfast for a week so you can afford it. How can you use resources available to you to the fullest extent with the time you're given?"

In coaching, the key to focus is – you guessed it – asking great questions (skill three is really important)! Instead of asking yourself (or your team), "why can't you figure this out?", try asking, "what haven't you thought of?"

The human brain is an incredibly powerful machine, but it won't 'autocorrect' your choice of words. Your brain will answer exactly the question you ask it. If you ask, 'why can't I figure it out?', you are *telling* your brain that you can't figure it out, and then asking for a reason why. When we ask questions like this, we get answers like, 'because you're just not that smart', or 'you're lazy and you give up easily', or 'you're an imposter and you don't know what you're doing'.

Our focus begins with how we frame the questions we ask ourselves and our team. As it relates to helping our team focus on opportunities, or finding great new strategies, we can ask better coaching questions like;

1. What is the best idea you all have to grow the business (for example)?

2. Who have we not talked to that could give us a fresh perspective?
3. If this was your business, and you needed to make it work, what would you do?
4. Where have we not looked?
5. Who is already doing what we are trying to do, and what can we learn from them?
6. What are our greatest strengths, and how can we leverage those in creative ways to reach our goals?
7. What does our purpose and vision compel us to do in this situation?

These are all example questions to get your synapses firing. Remember that the more present you are (skill five), the easier it is for brilliant questions to come to you organically as you listen to your team to understand (skill four).

Once we get our team's gray matter working, no doubt you will have plenty of new ideas to choose from. Typically, budgets, core competencies, timelines, and organizational objectives act as filters for what strategies we should or should not pursue. Chances are, as a business leader, you are not reading a book on coaching skills to learn how to choose the right strategy, that's probably already in your wheelhouse (at least it is for 94.2% of our survey respondents).

One last point on focus. Whatever you focus on grows. If you focus on problems, you will see more of them, and they will seem more severe. The more you focus on opportunities, the more of them you will see, and the more you'll start to detect them earlier than others.

When it comes to beliefs, what we believe to be possible affects how likely we are to take any given action. Our next skill involves a method to help your team understand their beliefs, and how beliefs are tied to the actions we take. Again, our actions dictate our results – so read on to learn how to unleash your team's best actions!

Skill Twelve: *Galvanize commitment and action*

Once we have our teams' individual and collective interests aligned, and our best course of action identified, the next logical step for any coach is to help move your team to decisive action. After all, why would anyone hire a fitness, nutrition, boxing, or executive coach if not to get better? At the professional level, you could argue that sport coaches are there to win championships, but at every level, they are there to make their players (and fellow coaches) better. Better performance. That's the end result of a professional who has worked with a great coach. That's your job as a leader – make your team better. For our purposes, by 'better', we don't just mean better results. A task master might grind their team harder and harder to achieve better results in the short run, only to suffer burnout and high employee turnover in the long run. As coaches, we achieve better results by building more capability and commitment in our teams. That's sustainable success.

Bringing us back to the focus of this chapter, our next coaching skill is all about galvanizing commitment and action. Basically, understanding how to be a catalyst for your team(s) to help them take more, better action(s).

While beyond both the scope of practice, and the job description, of leaders in business – the fundamental theory behind cognitive behavioral therapy (CBT) works wonders to help coaches (and those we coach) understand how to take more (and better) action(s). In short, rather than how we might think about our emotions (a bad thing happened and so we are in a bad mood),

CBT separates events, emotions, and adds a cause-and-effect relationship.

A trigger event (any event) happens, and in CBT theory, the event is neutral; neither good nor bad. Given that we have between 86 billion and 100 billion (100,000,000,000) neurons[26], and that we have over 6,000 thoughts per day[27], we have thoughts about everything that happens in our lives. An event happens, after which we have a thought. In CBT theory, our thoughts inform our beliefs. Imagine your new hire is late for work on their first day. You likely have a plethora of thoughts. Maybe you give them the benefit of the doubt, maybe traffic was bad. If they're late on day two, you're probably down to a few thoughts: my new hire is tardy, or my new hire is unprofessional, even disrespectful. Maybe you even think you made the wrong hire. That's how fast thoughts can become beliefs.

Think of beliefs as the sidelines of the possible. You wouldn't step on stage as a comedian if no one ever laughed at one of your jokes, and you might not try out for the hockey team if you have never skated and are afraid of getting hit. Because our beliefs frame what we think is possible, they heavily affect, if not dictate, our emotional state. In either of the above examples, both people might feel like a failure before they even tried. They might feel hopeless, or victimized ("why me?").

Our emotions dictate what action(s) we do or don't take. We go to the gym when we feel motivated. We cash out our investments when we feel panic. We lash out and blame our significant others for wronging us when we feel resentful. You get the point.

The last piece of CBT theory postulates that our actions (or lack thereof) dictate our results. I like to use a stock market crash to demonstrate CBT at work. The S & P 500 contracts by, let's say, 10% in a day. This may lead an entrepreneur to think that it's a 'bad economy'. They might develop the belief that businesses are doomed, which may lead to emotions of hopelessness, despair, and even depression. From this emotional state, said entrepreneur would not be inspired to reach out to potential customers, pitch investors for seed capital, or do much of anything. They might even close their doors for good.

Let's bring it back to you. Committed action is the end game. Quality strategies deployed with quality execution, consistently. How do you get your team there? What emotions would lead to the volume and quality of action you're hoping they undertake?

Some action-inducing emotions include invigorated, excited, passionate, committed, zealous, energized, motivated, and purposeful. What beliefs could cause such powerful emotions? Of course, there could be many different beliefs that lead to these positive emotions. In general, positive beliefs would lead to these positive emotions, and positive actions.

Remember skill three? Asking profound questions. Here are some examples of profound questions that can help uncover your teams' thoughts, beliefs, and emotions:

1. Jeff, what do you think we can achieve next year in terms of top line revenue growth if our team performs at their best?
2. Muhammad, how do you feel about our ability to execute the plan?
3. Cindy, what do you think is possible for you next year?
4. Meredith, on a scale of 1 to 10, how close are you to feeling your best?
5. Francois, what do you believe we can do as a company about (x or y situation)?

You don't have to be a motivational coach, but expecting someone's best while they're at their worst isn't fair either.

Remember the saying, 'well begun is half done'. After that, the job becomes much easier. Follow up, ask profound questions, listen to understand, remember their values and currency, clarify expectations, and hold your team accountable to their commitments and deliverables. It's not rocket science – it's neuroscience!

In his 2022 book, 'The Earned Life', Marshall Goldsmith suggests two conditions necessary for leaders to help their teams take the feedback they've been given (skill nine) and use it to change their behavior (or performance) for good.

First, one is not done. That is, once the feedback has been given, regular, timely follow up is important to keep our teams on track[28]. Once feedback has been delivered and follow up on, the responsibility shifts to the team to bring their discipline and willpower to improving and sustaining their performance[28]. Skills six (uncovering their values and currency) and ten (aligning personal and organizational objectives) can go a long way to helping your team remember what is important, and thus increase their reservoir of both discipline and willpower.

Even when leaders do a masterful job of delivering and following up on feedback (while deploying all of the other skills), mistakes and mis-steps are inevitable. Our next section dives into what you as the leader-coach can do when this happens to course correct and get your team back to moving in the right direction.

Skill Thirteen: *Facilitate, don't fix.*

We have a saying in our business, "always a conduit, never a crutch". By this we mean that as leaders, our job is to help drive greater learning, awareness, and skill acquisition, thus better outcomes. Our job is not to do the work for our team, or rescue them if they haven't done the work themselves. As another old saying goes, 'give a man a fish and he'll eat for a day. Teach a man to fish and he'll feed for a lifetime.'

Sometimes this means doing less. For Nina Bouzamondo-Bernstein, it took a lot of growth to give more autonomy since she is such a doer. She often felt an urge to take over. She would feel compelled to send the Pre-Health Shadowing social media post if the person who was supposed to do it was late, however Nina warns "that makes people feel horrible". Even if the leader can do it faster, it's important for the team to learn and become more efficient. Give them the space to grow and support them through that growth.

Like Nina, it might take every ounce of restraint within you not to jump in and 'rescue' a team member who is really struggling. At the crux of this internal struggle are two competing desires we have as leaders;

1. We don't want to see our team struggle, or in pain of any kind
2. We *do* want to see our team thrive

In order to resolve this kind of conflict, leaders must ask themselves what kind of coach, and what kind of leader, they want to be. Do you want to be the kind of leader who protects their team from harm, or do you want to be the kind of leader who empowers your team for greatness?

It may not always be an 'either – or' proposition. When the urge to rescue (that comes from great care, if not love, of your team) sets in, the action you take next must be aligned with your purpose and vision as a leader. *What* you do next must be consistent with *why* you chose leadership, and *where* you are trying to lead your organization.

While we are careful not to sway your opinion, in our experience struggle is a far greater teacher than safety. Whichever direction you lean as a leader, we compel you to act in concert with what's best for your team, not just what satisfies your immediate emotional reaction. Remember the focus rule from the feedback section – it's about them, not about you.

Step in to help your team if they are struggling unnecessarily, or not learning through the process. Do not step in if you feel bad, or you are feeling uncomfortable. We've all heard the cliché that 'great things don't come from comfort zones'. In our experience, it's quite true.

Besides preventing your team from learning or becoming empowered, there's another important reason you as the leader can't step in every time your team struggles. When the team comes to you at the first sign of trouble, then the operation breaks down without you. As much as this might make a leader feel valued, it actually detracts value from the team and the organization. Instead of you becoming the 'irreplaceable leader' – you've just become the bottleneck. Rather than growing the team and the organization, you are slowing everything down. The organization can only move as fast as you can solve one problem at a time.

A common temptation for executive coaches is validation. It's tempting to show your client (or your team) how smart you are. Over time, most coaches realize there is a very low ceiling to being the smartest person in the room. You cap who you can work with, how much you can help them, and even your own earning potential. If we can embrace the notion that leadership and coaching is not about us, but about our team, we can be even more effective. Rather than creating value by imparting knowledge in others, we can create even more value by unlocking the wisdom within others. New Zealand's top executive coach Nick Roud reminds us that, "coaching isn't about fixing it's about enabling the coachee (person you are coaching) to really excel".

Empowerment builds others, and in doing so, builds capacity in the organization. It speeds the whole operation up as you the leader are no longer required to solve every problem. Many leaders struggle at this point, feeling less 'needed'. The hidden opportunity here is to evolve how you contribute value to your team and your organization. Rather than being a subject matter expert or a manager, you can become a coach – whose role it is to lift the potential of all of those around you, as well as the potential and the performance of the organization as a whole.

What kind of leader do you want to be? A 'fixer', or a 'facilitator'?

Skill Fourteen: *Reframe and rebuild*

As briefly touched upon in the previous section, things don't always go as planned. Building on the notion that a leaders' role is not to always 'fix' or 'do' for their team, that doesn't mean your job is to sit idly by watching them struggle until they 'get it'. While exercising restraint and refusing to 'step in and save' our team *is* one way of empowering them to solve their own challenges, there are other approaches you as their leader can take to help them get better results. Before we get there, don't discount the immense value all of us glean when we are left to solve our own problems. While the process may not be enjoyable, the learning is hard to mimic.

"We must learn from mistakes, because we're bound to make them" urges. Dr. Marilyn Taylor. She elaborates that "aspiring leaders often back away from messes or uncertainty because they don't want to look bad, but these are the very areas that leaders need to address the most. Whether we agree or not we have a deeper common responsibility". The focus needs to shift from 'me' to 'we', advises Taylor. "It's impossible to do this 100% of the time; it's natural we get self-absorbed at times, but greater attentiveness allows us the potential to be wise and act in our collective best interests".

Whether we step in to coach, or leave our team to learn through trial and error, there will be times things don't go as planned. In his book "Can't Hurt Me", David Goggins details a military strategy he's pulled into his personal development and consulting work – the after-action-review (AAR)[29]. In essence, the AAR is a debrief of any mission (or any critical task for that matter), designed to dissect what went well, and what can be learned and thus improved in future scenarios[29]. Translating the AAR into coaching terms, recall the CBT (cognitive behavioral therapy) framework from skill twelve. Outcomes are generally objective, and are thus a great place to start any sort of forensic investigation. You did or did not make your sales targets. You did or did not complete the project on time and/ or on budget. There were or were not any safety incidents in the field.

Remember that our actions lead to our results. Start by asking what strategies the team deployed. Stay curious; in other words – be present (skill five). Avoid judgement, and we can get to where the real discussion starts; the thoughts and emotions that led to the actions that were or were not taken.

In the world of psychology, limiting beliefs are often referred to as 'maladaptive beliefs'. That makes them sounds a bit more damaging than 'limiting beliefs', which can be positive if it leads to tackling the thinking behind a limiting belief instead of dismissing it. Diagnosing a limiting belief, especially in terms of psychological pathology, is not your job. One thing you can do is challenge limiting thinking. In the coaching world, we often do this through 'reframing'.

Reframing is different than being a public relations 'spin doctor' after a corporate scandal. Reframing is not calling a burned down house a 'fresh supply of carbon'. Reframing *is* helping your team see and choose a different perspective. An example would be challenging a frustrated team member's view that 'there's not opportunity here'. If the local economy is struggling, or no job postings for promotion are being posted, you as their coach might suggest this is a prime opportunity for them to be more proactive or creative. After all, a job posting invites applicants. No posting is a great time for driven individuals to draft a creative business proposal for a new role or a new revenue stream to pitch their supervisor.

Savvy entrepreneurs know that there is always more opportunity in times of chaos or disruption than there is during times of relative calm. It might not be the window of opportunity we would ask for, but an opportunity is an opportunity.

Examples of reframing negative thoughts into possibilities are below:

- "It's a terrible economy" can be reframed as "it's a great time to buy a depressed asset" or "taking action now could instill consumer confidence while your competitors try to hide in the shadows and ride out the storm"
- "I'm just not a salesperson" could be reframed as "you're not a snake oil salesperson. Most customers these days want authenticity, which means you could end up being our top sales professional!"
- "I've tried everything" can be reframed as "You've tried everything you've thought of. Who do you know that thinks wildly different than you? Pick their brain and maybe you'll have some fresh new ideas"
- "Dave is just impossible – there's no getting through to him" can be reframed as "Are you speaking Dave's language? Have you taken the time to discover Dave's

currency? Are you speaking to him from his viewpoint, or your own?"

- "Who am I to give the presentation at the board meeting? No one wants to hear from me, I'm not even a VP" can be reframed as "You've been asked for a reason. You're a high potential, and you see the company from a different perspective than the Board of Directors or Executive team. Your different opinion is your source of value – we don't want group think here!"

There are countless more examples, but rather than belabor the point, it's time to give you a chance to try your new skill of reframing. How would you reframe each of the following?

1. "I'm underpaid for what I'm worth"

2. "Our competitor's products are way better"

3. "I never have enough time in a day"

4. "Our new employees just don't get it"

By now you no doubt see a coach's role is not to tell your team what to think, but to challenge their thinking patterns when lower quality thoughts are potentially holding them back from greater happiness, performance, and growth. One question great coaches ask their clients when faced with limiting beliefs is, "do you have all of the proof you need to know that this is 100% true?"

Just like in the sciences, a lack of proof of your hypothesis means other possibilities must be considered. The extroverted sales professional who 'tried everything', but didn't think to reach out to the introverted operations manager who might help them with new strategies has to concede, "ok, I guess I haven't tried *everything*".

As a leader coach, you don't need to have all of the answers. As Ed Batista puts it, "it's unrealistic and ill-advised to expect them to have all the answers. Organizations are simply too complex for leaders to govern on that basis."[17] You don't need to be the smartest person in the room. This isn't 1982.

If you can get your team to consider other points of view, you've won. As Tim Grover points out in his book Winning, humans are inherently competitive, we want to win – just observe a young child who loses a race or a board game[30]. The same is true for your team. They want to win. Given new possibilities, new options, new hope – they will double down their efforts to get the job done. Your job is to help them get back onto their figurative playing field as the best version of themselves.

Reframe, and then rebuild the potential of the team in front of you – that's the leader coach's job!

Skill Fifteen: *Leaders create more leaders, not just followers*

At the crux of nearly every 'success bible' or success 'how-to' is the notion that it is not just about us. When it comes to leadership, it's clear; if not obvious that leadership is about those in the leaders' care. The truly great leaders, however- the best of the best- see further into the future than the rest of us.

If a good leader takes pride in coaching their team in order to lift them towards their potential; than a great coach teaches their team how to become coaches. Furthermore, they teach their team how to coach other coaches, so that their impact- no- *legacy* – will be measured over decades instead of years.

Central to adopting this long-term view is that the leader also has their scoreboard for success identified, and that other people's success is at the heart of their motivation. If money, title, status or power are the primary drivers for a leader, they will never become a great coach, let alone a mentor-coach of other coaches. Ironically, the more selfless a leader becomes, and the more people they lift toward their potential, the greater the individual rewards including recognition, opportunities, and financial rewards.

After all, what would quantify a 'great' coach more than the number of people that they helped become the best version of themselves?

Practically speaking, coaching a leader to coach others and create more leaders requires that extra long-range vision, as well as intention. You might have coached a leader using all 14 of the previous skills, to the point that they become a top performer. Your team might now be among the very best in their organization, if not their field. That being said, sometimes high performers experience a 'success bottleneck'. If your team ends up being the top performers in key roles, with no succession plan, then they are stuck in their roster spots and so is everyone 'below them' in the org chart.

As you coach Jen to be your top sales person, for instance, you will need to start asking her who she is grooming to replace herself. As Jen mentions how impactful your coaching to her has been, you might ask her who she is paying it forward to – who is she coaching?

The key to maintaining the focus of developing others who develop others – is to maintain the truth that coaching is about our teams, not about us. If coaching is just about you as the leader, then the goal of coaching might be to build and retain the best team around you. This is the kind of philosophy that leads team leaders to develop their teams to a point – and *then suppress them*!

Many so-called 'leaders' hold their teams back, intentionally or not, through several means;

1. Developing them until they are self-sufficient and then shifting their focus to the rest of their team. These leaders forget that an organization's top people love a challenge, and are the most likely next crop of future leaders.
2. Coercing or 'guilting' the leader into staying. "We've invested a lot in you – don't you think about leaving now".
3. The 'golden handcuffs'. Incentivizing senior leaders with stock options, LTI (long-term incentive) plans, or hefty bonuses to make it against their best interests to leave. We are not suggesting that these programs are inherently bad. It's important to reward performance and loyalty; we're just suggesting this should not just be a tactic to manipulate people to stay.
4. Passive or active 'ghosting'. Some 'leaders' actually start to disengage from their top people, rather than continuing to invest. They might say things like, "we know you're off to bigger and better things, so we're focusing on the rest of the team. Don't forget us 'little

people' when you're a big star on the cover of Forbes magazine big shot!"
5. Packaging senior leaders out early when they perceive the leader could become a threat to morale, intellectual property, or to steal the company's top clients.
6. Procrastinating or even denying their teams' leadership training. According to research, every year a company delays leadership training, it costs 7% of their total annual sales[31]. In almost all cases, this wasted expense totals far more than the budget for leadership training itself!

Instead, we prefer the approach that true servant leaders take. Recall Gene Smith's philosophy of "develop people so well that you lose some of them". In fact, at the time of our interview the leadership team of Ohio State's athletic department consisted of Smith and 12 other senior leaders. At that time, Smith confided he was going to invite five of his top performers to leave. This was not because of a drop in their performance, or behavior. It was because Smith knew it was time for these five to take the next steps in their careers and become athletic directors elsewhere. It's an example I've shared countless times with leaders who fear losing their best people. Do the right thing just because it's the right thing. Do what's right for them, not just yourself or your organization.

Suppressing others is not leadership; in fact, it's the opposite of leadership. Think of a leader who tried to hold you back, or who tried to hold on to you because it was the best thing for them, not for you. As a leader, you owe it to every leader who invested in you to pay it forward. As a leader, you owe it to every other great leader who came before you and cleared a path to keep fighting the good fight. As a leader who benefited along the way from others' selfless work, you owe it to them all to keep doing the right thing just because it's the right thing to do. As a former follower who was inspired along the way to lead, you owe it to your team, and everyone else watching your example, to look within others and see – and develop – their potential.

Leaders bring out the best in others, and when those others have the potential to lead others, it is your responsibility to make sure that the wisdom of all who have come before you does not stop with you. More simply – leave your organization and the people within it better than you found it.

Sometimes leaders don't see the results of their investment in others. Sometimes we need to trust that doing the right thing pays off even if we don't see it. Sometimes, we do get to see the results of our hard work. Gene Smith informed me that there were 22 African American Athletic Directors out of 130 Division One schools when we spoke. When he started as an Athletic Director, there were four. Smith says that he tried to create a pipeline, try to open doors for others in the top ranks of collegiate sports management. He's tried to impress this on others as well, especially African American Athletic Directors, to help eventually achieve true equality. Now *that* is leadership.

6

The DNA of tomorrow's leader

As much as this book has been my effort to contribute to the field of leadership, I have no delusions that this book becomes *the* evergreen handbook to training great leaders. The world is changing too much, too fast, and I don't think any of us expect that rate of change to somehow slow in the future. The goal has been to document just how much has changed, and what specifically has changed, to better equip leaders and organizations for success today, and over (I hope) the next 10 to 15 years.

William Arruda wrote an article for Forbes in May, 2023, "7 soft skills you should master to advance your career"[32]. In the advent of tools like ChatGPT and other AI (artificial intelligence) platforms, Arruda lists the following skills as ones AI will not be able to replace;

1. Self-awareness
2. Feedback
3. Emotional Intelligence
4. Listening
5. Inclusive leadership
6. Coaching
7. Virtual presence (how to 'show up' and participate in and lead effective meetings over Zoom or MS Teams)[32]

Now that we've broken down the skill gaps and trends for leaders exposed through our research and leader interviews, let's summarize them into what a leader prepared for tomorrow's challenges might behave like. In order to do so, it's useful to think of how we have defined leadership prowess in the past, and, as

William Arruda suggests, what leaders are being called to in the future.

Wayne Gretzky famously said that what made him a great hockey player was that he tried to ""skate to where the puck is going, not where it has been". As leaders and organizations trying to navigate life in the new organization of 2024 and beyond, this is the same task. The simplest lens I can present to compare is the lens through which leaders were, and will be, recognized.

Would you disagree that leaders have historically been measured on results? I think most of us would concur, after all, that's a pretty good place to start. The trap, however, with results-oriented praise and promotions, is that it is a model for perpetuating what has always worked. It's a recipe for 'more of the same', or 'skating to where the puck has been'. Remember the pace of change we discussed? Will more of the same somehow work the same (or better) in a new reality?

I would offer that the leader of tomorrow should be evaluated based on their ability to cultivate potential in others. This shift in priority may seem subtle, but let's compare what priorities and values a results-oriented leader, and a potential-oriented leader each focus on.

Results-focused leader	Potential-focused leader
Profit	Purpose
Achieving goals	Facilitating growth
Shareholder returns	Customer pain points
Knowledge	Wisdom
Having all the answers	Asking the right questions
Career advancement	Career development of others
Massive buyout	Legacy
Earning more	Helping more
The best strategy	How to ignite strategy through culture

Results will always matter. Leaders will always be measured by what they can accomplish, but what I hope this book can accomplish, is to have more business owners, CEOs, boards of directors, and future leaders see a bigger picture.

To stay committed to a bigger picture – a cause larger than oneself – is the epitome of purpose. To Sonny Melendrez, it's also important to have passion, or as he calls it, 'intentional enthusiasm'. To Sonny, intentional enthusiasm is one of the cornerstones to leadership, success, and a life of fulfillment. According to Melendrez, the three pillars of intentional enthusiasm are:

1. Belief in yourself. Remember, "you are going to become whatever it is you tell yourself that you are" so be kind and be positive in your thoughts about yourself.
2. Vision. "You have to have a clear vision for what it is that you want to accomplish".

3. Gratitude. The more grateful we are, the more abundance we see. It doesn't come from "I want or I need".

The first piece of advice Sister Simone Campbell gives for those new to or considering leadership is to figure out their mission. Campbell explains her leadership paradigm as a diamond, with mission and vision at the top; what is it? Where are you going?

Another important aspect of the diamond model, explains Campbell, is power. "Power is the decider, but we also have to understand what is the power of resistance?". In other words, what is working *against* you?

Sister Simone explains, "the third aspect is energy – the 'joie de vivre', and the fourth is structure: how it gets done, the making of committees, the chain of command, and so on."

Finally, "at the bottom is resources: money, materials, people, and resources – if we don't have enough – trickle up and impact mission. It's a connected cycle."

Figure 6.1: Sister Simone Campbell's diamond model of leadership

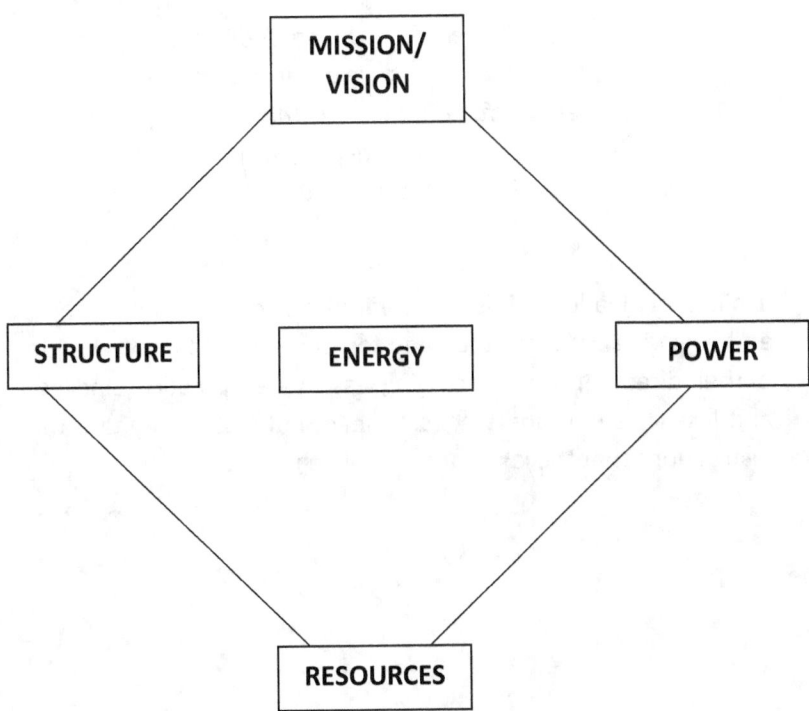

Campbell teaches a powerful lesson on leadership at work during conflict. "Everyone has a dominant corner, and that's where leaders go in struggle. The way to resolve power struggle is not arm wresting; it's by going to mission, and having a mission that's clear enough to make it worthwhile to shift the power balance."

I worked with a wise coach around 10 years ago, and I'll never forget his advice to me, which I now offer up to the same business owners, CEOs, boards of directors, and future leaders I hope to reach;

Business is just a platform for helping others. All you need to figure out is who you want to help.

The great paradox, as well as the great incentive, that I've seen in my 25 years in leadership, is this:

> *the more leaders focus on potential, the more they tend to produce great results. The more leaders focus on results, the more they 'lower the ceiling' on potential, which limits their long-term results.*

While every leader stands to benefit from 'on the job experience' and 'knowing the role', the need for the leader to know the job of their direct reports is becoming less and less practical, and less and less logical. Leaders need to lead, not just regurgitate the instructions that the last leader before them gave.

7

Call to action

Nina Bouzamonda-Bernstein reminds us that "leaders are doers". As an executive coach and business advisor focused on helping clients take decisive action to see better results – I couldn't agree more. This means you have homework; after all, if I wanted to write books just for entertainment purposes, I'd write fiction. As leaders, it will take all of us to solve the problems we've discussed throughout this book, and leave the world better for the next wave of leaders.

If you are an athlete, and your coach told you exactly what you needed to do to make the team, or receive an athletic scholarship – I bet you would do it. Leadership development is no different.

If you are an emerging leader, consider the 15 skills described in this book as your homework. Learn them, practice them, and seek feedback from your peers, supervisors, and direct reports. Find out how you are doing in applying these skills, and set whatever goals make sense to you based on your purpose and career aspirations to keep improving these skills.

If you are a senior leader, your homework is to reflect, and seek feedback, on your leadership game. There is no place on any org chart that the leader is above reflection, feedback, or growth. Next, your homework is to learn the skills outlined in this book well enough to be able to teach others (remember skill 15), and support your emerging leaders along their journey. It is your role to shift your organization from a focus on results – to a focus on potential.

In either case, we have taken the skills outlined in this book and in the State of Leadership Readiness Survey and created a leadership course called Leadership That LASTS (Leadership Acceleration and Succession Training System). The course can be accessed at https://getsuccessfaster.com/leadership-that-lasts/

Perhaps you work in human resources, talent development, or people and culture. Your homework is to review your leadership infrastructure. Review your leadership attraction, recruitment, onboarding, and development systems. If you don't have them, start building them. If they aren't meeting your organizations' performance goals, improve them. If you don't know how you're doing, start measuring. What gets measured gets accomplished. Be part of the solution by investing in your leaders; time, skill development, coaching, training, mentorship, and whatever else your leaders need to become multipliers.

Finally, if you are an educator, in an academic or a corporate setting – become a trailblazer. Take a page out of Dr. Marilyn Taylor's book and find ways of combining validated research with innovation. Stick with what works, and try new things, or you risk repeating the mistakes of the past as highlighted in chapter two.

If we expect our teams to develop a 'no job is beneath me' attitude, then we as leaders have to leave no stone unturned when it comes to creating the best environment possible for their growth and development. That is the homework of all true leaders: never stop trying to leave those we serve better than we found them. It is a race with no finish line, but there is no better feeling than to know that others' lives are better because of you.

> Let's stop racing towards 'perfecting leadership'.
>
> Now is the time for fixing leadership.

Appendix A: Leaders full biographies

Gary Bertwistle

Gary has always had a passion for innovation, creativity and doing things differently. His career has spanned the retail, music, media, corporate education and radio industries. Gary's greatest desire comes from having people and organizations think differently to find new ways of doing things…. to break the status quo and redesign the traditional formula. Gary has helped companies, teams and individuals in companies of all sizes, in all industries and categories, to look at how they currently do things and address what needs to change in order for them to think differently and maximize their potential. He is often called upon when companies or individuals lose their mojo. He has also built a reputation for his ability to interview the world's foremost thinkers in every aspect of life and business on his podcasts to curate the learnings gained there and distill them into usable and practical advice about how to get our mojo working.

Through easy to understand, fun, interactive virtual and live keynote speeches, he presents to a wide variety of clients globally in the areas of performance, strategic mojo, personal mojo, marketing warfare and innovation to improve performance and help individuals be at their best. His work is helping companies and leaders unlock great ideas to get their mojo working.

Gary's Portfolio of Work:

- Opened Australia's first ever creative thinking venue, The Ideas Vault, in Sydney
- Won the TEC Speaker of the Year in 2007, 2008 and again in 2012

- Built a catalogue of over 300 interviews with the worlds' foremost thinkers.
- Published 6 books including the best sellers: *Who Stole My Mojo?* and *The Vibe*
- Publishes a weekly blog for thinkers, called The Espresso
- Co-founded Australia's leading cycling foundation, the Tour de Cure and raised over $118 million for Cancer research, support, and prevention
- Successfully launched a Kickstarter campaign for The Mojo Journal, the world's first thought provoking journal.
- Australian of Year Finalist 2018
- Deputy Captain, Rural Fire Service
- Host of [The Mojo Sessions podcast](), featuring intimate conversations with the world's most interesting people.

Nina Bouzamondo-Bernstein

Founder and CEO of Pre-Health Shadowing, an organization of more than 4,700 student volunteers who have helped more than 60,000 pre-health students from around the world gain access to medical, dental, nursing, pharmaceutical and other health shadowing hours. Nina and her team have helped pre-health students earn over 164,000 certificates and designations. Nina is also an advisory board member, women in leadership, at California State Polytechnic University.

Nina and Pre-Health Shadowing have been featured on KCSB News Radio, UC Santa Barbara Magazine, and KSEE24 Television News. Across their various social media channels, Pre-Health Shadowing has amassed over 20,000 followers in less than four years.

Sister Simone Campbell

Sister Simone Campbell served as Executive Director of NETWORK Lobby for Catholic Social Justice from 2004-2021. She is a religious leader, attorney and poet with extensive experience in public policy and advocacy for systemic change. In Washington, she lobbies on issues that help "mend the gaps" in income and wealth in the U.S., focused specifically on how they disproportionately affect people of color and women. Around the country, she is a noted speaker and educator on these public policy issues.

During the 2010 congressional debate about healthcare reform, she wrote the famous "nuns' letter" supporting the reform bill and organized 59 leaders of Catholic Sisters, including the Leadership Conference of Women Religious (LCWR), to sign on. This action was cited by many as critically important in passing the Affordable Care Act. She was thanked by President Obama and invited to the ceremony celebrating its being signed into law.

In 2012, she was also instrumental in organizing the first "Nuns on the Bus" tour to oppose the "Ryan Budget" approved by the House of Representatives. This budget would decimate programs meant to help people in need. "Nuns on the Bus" received an avalanche of attention across the nation from religious communities, elected officials, and the media.

Since then, Sister Simone Campbell has led six cross-country "Nuns on the Bus" trips, focused on tax justice, healthcare, economic justice, comprehensive immigration reform, voter turnout, bridging divides in politics and society, and mending the gaps in wealth and access in our nation. In 2020, Sister Simone led the first virtual Nuns on the Bus tour, completing 63 virtual events in the weeks leading up to the 2020 Election.

Sister Simone has often been featured in the national and international media, including appearances on 60 Minutes, The Colbert Report, and The Daily Show with Jon Stewart.

She has received numerous awards, including the "Franklin D. Roosevelt Four Freedoms Award" and the "Defender of Democracy Award" from the international Parliamentarians for Global Action. Additionally, she has been the keynote or featured speaker at numerous large gatherings, including both the 2012 and 2020 Democratic National Conventions.

Prior to coming to NETWORK, Simone served as the Executive Director of JERICHO, the California interfaith public policy organization that works like NETWORK to protect the interests of people living in poverty. Simone also participated in a delegation of religious leaders to Iraq in December 2002, just prior to the war, and was later (while at NETWORK) part of a Catholic Relief Services delegation to Lebanon and Syria to study the Iraqi refugee situation there.

Before JERICHO, Simone served as the general director of her religious community, the Sisters of Social Service. She was the leader of her Sisters in the United States, Mexico, Taiwan and the Philippines. In this capacity, she negotiated with government and religious leaders in each of these countries.

In 1978, Simone founded and served for 18 years as the lead attorney for the Community Law Center in Oakland, California. She served the family law and probate needs of the working poor of her county.

She is also the author of Hunger for Hope, published September 2020 by Orbis Books, and A Nun on the Bus: How All of Us Can Create Hope, Change, and Community, published April 2014 by HarperCollins.

Lieutenant-General M.A.J. Carignan

A graduate of the Royal Military College of Canada in Engineering, Lieutenant-General Jennie Carignan was commissioned into the Canadian Military Engineers in 1990. Since then, she commanded two Combat Engineer Regiments, Royal Military College Saint-Jean and the 2nd Canadian Division, where she led more than 10,000 soldiers and spearheaded crisis operations during the flood relief efforts in the spring of 2019 in Quebec. More recently, she led NATO Mission Iraq from November 2019 to November 2020. LGen Carignan participated in three previous expeditionary operations in Bosnia-Herzegovina, the Golan Heights, and Afghanistan. Along the way, LGen Carignan earned a Master's degree in Business Administration from Université Laval and a second Master's degree from the United States Army Command and General Staff College and the School of Advanced Military Studies. She is also a graduate of the National Security Studies Programme from Canadian Forces College in Toronto.

LGen Carignan has been invested as Commander of the Order of Military Merit and is the recipient of the Meritorious Service Medal. She received the prestigious Gloire de l'Escolle medal which recognizes graduates from Université Laval who have distinguished themselves professionally and in service to their communities. She was recently awarded an honorary doctorate in Business Administration from Université Laval. LGen Carignan was promoted to her current rank in April of 2021 and appointed as Chief of Professional Conduct and Culture, a newly created position in the CAF.

Married, Jennie is the mother of four children, two of whom proudly serve in the Canadian Armed Forces.

Ruth Glenn

Ms. Ruth M. Glenn is the President/CEO of the National Coalition Against Domestic Violence, as well as the President of Public Affairs for both the NCADV and the National Domestic Violence Hotline.

Previously, Ms. Glenn was employed by the Colorado Department of Human Services for 28 years and served as the Director of the Domestic Violence Program (DVP) for the last nine of those years. Ruth has worked and volunteered in the domestic violence field for over 20 years and holds a Masters' in Public Administration (MPA) from the University of Colorado Denver, Program on Domestic Violence, as well as a degree in Communications.

Ms. Glenn has served on many domestic violence program and funding boards, provided hundreds of presentations on domestic violence victimization and survival, testified before the Colorado state legislature and the United States Congress, and provided consultation, training and technical assistance on a local and national level on victim/survivor issues as they relate to domestic violence. As a survivor, Ruth also shares her experience to bring awareness about the dynamics of domestic violence. She also intends to continue to tell her story to encourage and empower others to raise their voices about their experiences.

Ruth released her memoir, Everything I Never Dreamed, in 2022. Her book became a bestseller on Amazon, and was featured in several prominent publications, including the Wall Street Journal.

Nicole Jansen

There are few people who can captivate both a small group of 15 and inspire a large group of 3000 with a message that touches them all deeply.

As a business owner and entrepreneur for over 30 years Nicole Jansen has helped thousands of leaders and organizations earn millions of dollars by bringing massive value to the marketplace. Her deep passion for helping people discover their greatness and live life at the next level is what has made her one of the most in-demand speakers and coaches in her region.

Her message is one of empowerment, focus, and relentless commitment to being the best you can be; that the road to success is paved with conscious awareness, inspired action, and fostering meaningful connections with others.

Nicole is passionate about empowering motivated leaders with proven business development skills as well as the necessary self-awareness to master "the little voice in their head" and create the outcomes they desire. It is this combination of personal and business mastery that has earned Nicole the reputation of helping her clients and audiences achieve incredible results in such a short period of time. Very few understand how to blend these skills together to create the magic that she creates for others.

In addition to her 30+ years of experience in business, sales, leadership, training and coaching, Nicole is certified with the following designations:

- Human Behavior Specialist, Personality Insights and Kolbe Corp.
- Strategic Intervention Coach, Robbins-Madanes Training
- Business Coach & Trainer, SalesPartners Worldwide
- Master Facilitator, Blair Singer Training

Through Nicole's breakthrough coaching and training, her clients enjoy greater clarity, confidence and capacity, as well as breakthrough results including:

- ✓ Increased sales 150% in 4 weeks
- ✓ Doubling revenue year over year
- ✓ Increased profitability 2.5 times in 2 months
- ✓ Increased team sales activity 500% in one week
- ✓ Increased overall team performance 25% in 2 months

...all within the context of a healthy team environment where mission comes first, diversity is celebrated, and customer satisfaction is paramount.

Nicole enjoys meeting new people, traveling and expanding her vision, as well as surrounding herself with inspirational leaders who are using their strengths to positively transform lives around the world.

She is the founder of Discover The Edge, host of the Leaders Of Transformation Podcast, and co-author of the book, Power Up, Super Women.

Arturo Lomeli

Arturo is the founder of Clase Azul tequila, and the Fundacion Causa Azul. Clase Azul is considered by many experts to be the world's most luxurious tequila. The foundation helps Mexican artisans legitimize their craft and sell their art and creations through proper distribution channels rather than needing to sell on the streets or tourist beaches of Mexico.

After buying a bar at the age of 23, Arturo discovered that he didn't love the business, but he did discover a love for the spirits he sold. His first business 'failed miserably' in Arturo's words, but after studying marketing and learning the importance of differentiation, Arturo launched Clase Azul which has become a symbol for quality in the tequila and spirits business. In fact, they launched a $1,200 bottle of tequila in 2007 to "cause a stir" in the tequila market; more of a promotional stunt than anything, but it caught on and Clase Azul now has a $30,000 bottle of ultra anejo (extra aged) tequila[39].

Sonny Melendrez

Sonny Melendrez is in the business of inspiration. Motivating others has always been an important element in the life of this dynamic radio and television personality, author and inspirational speaker.

Twice named Billboard Magazine's "National Radio Personality of the Year," his enthusiasm for life is evident as host of local and national radio and television programs. He was presented the National Hispanic Radio Personality of the Year Award by Ricardo Montalban, then president of the National Nosotros Organization. In 2003, he was inducted into the Texas Radio Hall Of Fame and is included in the Rock & Roll Hall of Fame as one of the Top 100 Radio Personalities of All-Time.

Melendrez has served as program director and entertained at some of America's greatest radio stations, including KIIS, KMPC, KFI, KMGG, and KRLA in Los Angeles and KTSA, KTFM, KSMG, and KLUP in San Antonio. Under his leadership, these stations enjoyed stellar ratings and received countless awards for public service. His weekly radio show features the inspiring stories of celebrity guests from the world of entertainment.

Blessed with multiple talents, Sonny is equally at home as a TV host, actor, radio personality, writer, commercial spokesman, motivational speaker, or voice artist. He has served as TV and radio spokesperson for companies like Disney, Pepsi, McDonald's, Sears and Sprint.

As a motivational speaker and master of ceremonies, he has presented at such prestigious events as the White House Hispanic Heritage Awards (7 times); the National "Just Say No To Drugs" Rally at the Washington Monument; and the USO 50th Anniversary Gala at the Ambassador's Palace in Paris, France with guest of honor, the late Princess Grace of Monaco.

As host of the award-winning children's television series, "You and Me, Kid!" on the Disney Channel, Sonny enjoyed one of the longest runs in the network's history.

He was named Inc. Magazine's "Socially Responsible Entrepreneur of the Year," awarded the "Marketing Philanthropist Lifetime Achievement Award" by the Sales and Marketing Executives of San Antonio and named Alignable's 2017 San Antonio Small Business Person of the Year.

As the Los Angeles commissioner of the United Nation's Year of the Child, Melendrez was invited to Washington, D.C. to present his idea for a national children's holiday. Sunshine Day was officially proclaimed and celebrated in all 50 states on August 19th of that year, encouraging parents to spend the day, with their children, giving them what they most want and need: time and love.

The City of San Antonio named the Sonny Melendrez Community Center in his honor to say "thank you" for his community involvement, benefiting disadvantaged youth and families, including over 1400 motivational school presentations.

President Ronald Reagan commended Sonny for his efforts in the war on drugs and he received the National Director's Community Leadership Award by FBI Director, William S. Sessions. The Department of Justice lauded him with the prestigious "Modern Hero Award" for his efforts to inspire the nation's youth to "Soar In School". In recognition of raising tens of thousands of dollars for youth scholarships, he was named "El Rey Feo" (The People's King) and presided over San Antonio's annual weeklong Fiesta celebration.

Programs that benefit children have always been a priority for Sonny Melendrez. One of the projects of which he is most proud is The Children of the World Project, giving talented youth and countless volunteers a way to give back by recording the children's version of "We Are The World," which he created in Los Angeles in 1985. Over 1500 children participated in the recording and video and proceeds from record sales benefited USA for Africa. Sonny received a Grammy nomination for "Best Children's Recording."

There is hardly a charity or cause in San Antonio and many nationally, that has not received a helping hand from Sonny Melendrez. It's estimated that he has been responsible for raising over 100 million dollars in cash, goods and services for local and national non-profits during his career!

As a public servant, he's played a major role in countless city, county and state projects in the past 25 years, including his service as Bexar County Chairman of the 2010 Census.

A man of a thousand voices, he provided the voices of several characters in Hanna-Barbera's "Jetsons" cartoon series; created many of the sounds heard in the Gremlins Movie; played opposite Walter Mathau as the voice of Bob Cratchet in the animated TV classic, "The Stingiest Man in Town"; and was even the voice of the infamous Fred the Cockatoo in the 70"s NBC TV series, Baretta. He was chosen from a field of over 140,000 as the new voice of the Parkay Margarine Talking Tub, and after a nationwide search, Sonny was picked as voice of Jerry Seinfeld for a campaign promoting the Bee Movie Game for ActiVision.

Conferences, companies, colleges, universities, school districts, and groups of all types have been inspired by Sonny's captivating motivational presentations. His topics are designed to fire up companies, teachers, students, and parents to get involved and make a difference in the world around them, while delivering above-and-beyond service.

In his popular book, "The Art of Living with Enthusiasm!", Sonny presents the benefits to be found in positive living through personal and powerful stories of encouragement, comfort, and joy.

Nick Roud

Nick Roud has been named the #1 executive coach in all of New Zealand in 2019, 2020, and 2023. He is the founder of the leadership coaching company of the year 2022/23 at the Global Business Awards.

Nick Roud is one of the world's top executive coaches and a dedicated philanthropist. He has the highest-level coaching qualification (MCEC) Master Certified Executive Coach accredited by The International Coach Federation (ICF). Nick has personally coached over 1,000 executives and emerging leaders.

Nick also has several other certifications and credentials, including:

- 2022, RLA and RLA360 (Roud Leadership Assessments)
- 2022, Leadership Programme – Institute for Strategic Leadership, New Zealand
- 2017, Master Certified Executive Coach, Intelligent Leadership Executive Coaching, Accredited by The International Coach Federation, Global.
- 2017, Advanced MLEI Certified, Mattone Leadership Enneagram Inventory, Global.
- 2017, CPI260 Certified, CPP Asia Pacific, Global.
- 2017, Advanced STLI360 Certified, Global.
- 2016, MBTI Practitioner (Myers Briggs), CPP Asia Pacific, Global.
- 2016, Institute of Directors (IOD)
- Pro bono coaching Dyslexia Foundation of New Zealand
- Pro bono coaching International Coach Federation (ICF)

Gene Smith

Senior Vice President and Wolfe Foundation Endowed Athletic Director
The Ohio State University

Gene Smith is in his 18th year as director of athletics at The Ohio State University. Hired in 2005, he was promoted to Senior Vice President and Wolfe Foundation Endowed Athletics Director in May of 2016. Smith is only the eighth athletics director in Ohio State history, and he has the third-longest tenure in the position behind only L.W. St. John and Richard Larkins.

Ohio State's student-athletes continue to excel in the classroom and on the fields of play under the leadership of Smith, who directs the nation's largest and one of its elite athletic programs.

Smith is proud of the high-performance culture that has developed with the leadership of what he often refers to as "the best coaches and support staff in America." Record achievements by individuals, teams, and the entire athletic program attest to Ohio State's commitment to the development of the total student-athlete in a holistic way.

As the institution's academic profile has increased, so too has the academic profile of its student-athletes. In the classroom, student-athletes continue to distinguish themselves with record numbers earning university, conference, and national honors. Last year, Ohio State boasted a record 788 OSU Scholar-Athletes, 552 Academic All-Big Ten honorees and 213 student-athletes earned their degrees.

During Smith's tenure, Ohio State has dominated Big Ten Conference play, with 110 team and 346 individual conference championships. Nothing pleases Smith more than seeing student-athletes proudly display their championship rings – forever a reminder of their Ohio State experience.

On the national stage, Ohio State teams have won 28 team and 105 individual national championships during Smith's tenure, a mark of competitive excellence, and collected 1,422 All-America honors. In doing so, Ohio State has established itself as a perennial Top 5 contender in the Learfield Director's Cup. In 2021-22, the Buckeyes finished 4th.

Smith, a former student-athlete and coach, keeps a keen focus on the more than 1,000 student-athletes he serves. He is driven to provide for them all they need to grow academically, athletically, and socially during their time at Ohio State, and graduate with skills that transfer to success in life. Smith's focus on "recruitment to career" is evidenced in this year's graduating seniors with over 94% of them moving right into jobs, graduate school, or professional sports.

The Eugene D. Smith Leadership Institute – funded by private support – provides leadership, character, and career development for all Ohio State student-athletes to best prepare them for life after graduation. Institute programs include Bucks Go Pro internships, job shadows/micro-internships, Buckeye road trip, career fairs, Sundays in the Shoe, and Lead Like a Buckeye, among others.

Smith's business acumen has resulted in strong fiscal performance and new resources have been used to enhance the student-athlete experience. Record setting third party agreements – with NIKE, LEARFIELD, LEVY and COKE, among others – have allowed for innovative and trend setting programs offered to student-athletes.

Fund raising is one of Smith's gifts, and along with his development team, he has recently raised more than $150 million for the construction of the Schumaker Complex, Covelli Arena and Jennings Wrestling Center, Ty Tucker Tennis Center, and Lacrosse Stadium which became ready for competition in 2023.

Smith's duties extend beyond the athletic department as he also leads Ohio State's Business Advancement unit comprised of the Schottenstein Center, Nationwide Arena, Trademark & Licensing, Affinity Agreements, Drake Event Center, Blackwell Inn and Fawcett Center. Smith's team has increased revenues through innovation, collaboration and operational efficiencies.

Smith oversees a total of 486 employees in athletics and business advancement, with an annual budget of $315 million, and a football program with a $1.5 billion valuation, as estimated by the Wall Street Journal. But what Smith is most proud of is the exemplary culture within his units, recognized by Forbes as "one of the best ten organizations to work for in sports" and the only college program on its list.

After 38 years serving in the role of athletics director, Smith still delights in ensuring the student-athlete experience at Ohio State is exemplary and that its high-performance culture truly inspires young men and women to achieve their vast potential.

Smith currently serves on the Boards of Directors of the Columbus Sports Commission, Fiesta Bowl, National Football Foundation and Champions of Community. He is on the NCAA's Name, Image and Likeness Review Committee, and is active with NACDA (National Association of Collegiate Directors of Athletics).

Smith grew up in Cleveland and attended the University of Notre Dame on a football scholarship. He played four years as defensive end for the Irish and was a member of their 1973 Associated Press national championship team.

Smith received his bachelor's degree in business administration from Notre Dame in 1977. He joined the Notre Dame coaching staff following graduation, under Dan Devine, and coached four seasons. He helped Notre Dame win the 1977 national championship.

Smith is the father of four children with his wife, Sheila: Matt, Nicole, Lindsey, and Summer, and they are grandparents to eight: Marshall, Steele, Addison, Grayson, Tyson, Elijah, Maya, and Jordyn. Outside of work Smith enjoys travel, golf, and spending time with family.

Dr. Marilyn Taylor

Taylor joined Royal Roads in 2006 as a professor in the School of Leadership Studies. She is co-developer of the Executive Leadership specialization, MA in Leadership. She was the program head and developer of the Certificate in Values Based Leadership from 2011 to 2019, and director of the Institute for Values Based Leadership from 2008 to 2012. Prior to Royal Roads, Taylor was a professor at Concordia University for 23 years. At Concordia, she served as chair of the Department of Applied Social Science and director of the Centre for Human Relations and Community Studies; she was a key designer of the Master of Arts in Human Systems Intervention.

Taylor holds certifications and qualifications as follows:

- Qualification as Trainer of Consultant Certification for Culture Transformation Tools
- Certification in Cultural Transformation Tools – levels I & II, Practitioner, Barrett Values Centre
- Qualification in the Strength Deployment Inventory, Personal Strengths Publishing
- Graduate Certificate in Organizational Psychology with a concentration in Executive Coaching, Professional School of Psychology, Sacramento, California
- Qualification in Myers Briggs Type Indicator, Psychometrics Canada

Acknowledgements

Nothing, and I mean nothing great happens without a team. I have a lot of amazing people to thank who helped bring this book (a dream of mine) to the world.

First of all, thank you to everyone who reads this book, and answers my call to action – it will take all of us to fix the problems facing leadership today.

Thank you for taking the time to read Fixing Leadership in its' more primitive state, and yet leave such kind remarks Marshall Goldsmith, Rod Miller, Robb Holman, Michael Palmer, Patricia van De Sande, Matteo Borgna, and Brian Hughes.

Thank you to EMCC Global – the research in this book was able to reach a lot more leaders and coaches in a lot more places by allowing me to integrate the research into my closing Keynote address at your 2022 Global Conference. Thank you also to Harvard Business School online, which gave me the platform to reach many more leaders around the world to complete the State of Leadership Training Survey.

Thank you to all of the leaders and coaches who took the time to complete this survey, which helped bring the problems this book discusses to light – this book wouldn't have happened without you!

To the amazing leaders I had the luxury of interviewing for this book; Gary Bertwistle, Nina Bouzamondo-Bernstein, Sister Simone Campbell, LGen Jennie Carignan, Ruth Glenn, Nicole Jansen, Arturo Lomeli, Sonny Melendrez, Nick Roud, Gene Smith, and Dr. Marilyn Taylor; how can I possibly say thank you properly? You have each made me a better leader, made me set my sights higher, and my hope is that together – this book becomes OUR legacy.

To my amazing team of coaches at FSQ Consulting – thank you for the work you do every day to make leaders' lives better, and for making me a better coach and leader! To my amazing cofounders at FSQ – Matt Young, Taryn Lipschitz, and Nelson Soh – you make me better at what I do, you make the journey more enjoyable, and you make me a better person. 'Gratitude' doesn't come close to describing how I feel about you.

And as usual, last but far from least – my family. Thank you to my parents for being my first mentors and setting such a great example, my brother for setting the bar so low that I will always be the favorite, and my extended family for your constant support. The most important team I'll ever play for is the one I come home to every night. I hope to 'Fix Leadership' for the world, but more importantly, Maria and Chase I hope I've been the husband and father you deserve.

References

1. https://www.thesalesexperts.com/21-shocking-sales-facts-that-will-change-how-you-sell-forever/
2. https://www.forbes.com/sites/chriswestfall/2019/06/20/leadership-development-why-most-programs-dont-work/?sh=5ecdb05e61de
3. https://www.prnewswire.com/news-releases/corporate-leadership-training-market-size-to-grow-by-usd-15-78-bn--technavio-301515001.html
4. InfoPro infographic: https://www.infoprolearning.com/infographic/13-shocking-leadership-development-statistics-infopro-learning/
5. Pengue, Maria. *Leadership Statistics: Training, Demographics, and COVID-19*. Aug 11, 2021. www.writersblocklive.com
6. Hughes, Michael. *Companies are Overlooking a Primary Area for Growth and Efficiency: Their Managers*. March 2018 report. www.westmonroe.com
7. https://www.bloomberg.com/news/articles/2023-07-18/employees-are-stressed-by-inexperienced-first-time-managers?utm_source=website&utm_medium=share&utm_campaign=linkedin#xj4y7vzkg
8. Barrett, Richard. The New Leadership Paradigm. Lulu.com. 2010
9. Burlingham, Bo. Message in a bottle https://www.forbes.com/sites/boburlingham/2020/05/12/message-in-a-bottle-how-clase-azul-celebrates-mexican-culture-with-handcrafted-tequila-and-decanters/?sh=1dbf809f5e3e Forbes Magazine May 12, 2020
10. https://en.wikipedia.org/wiki/Simone_Campbell

11. Maxwell, John C. LeaderShift. Haper-Collins. 2019
12. Segal, Jeanne. The Language of Emotional Intelligence. McGraw-Hill. 2008
13. Mathers, Kate. *Threat or Reward – the over-arching organising principle of the brain*. Dec 22, 2017. https://www.iecl.com/threat-or-reward/#:~:text=The%20brain%20is%20always%20searching,second%2C%20below%20our%20conscious%20awareness.
14. https://www.ccl.org/articles/leading-effectively-articles/what-is-psychological-safety-at-work/
15. https://www.prochange.com/transtheoretical-model-of-behavior-change
16. Hall KL, Rossi JS. Meta-analytic examination of the strong and weak principles across 48 health behaviors. Prev Med. 2008 Mar;46(3):266-74. doi: 10.1016/j.ypmed.2007.11.006. Epub 2007 Nov 22. PMID: 18242667.
17. Batista, Ed. *How Great Coaches Ask, Listen, and Empathize*. Harvard Business Review. Feb 18, 2015 https://hbr.org/2015/02/how-great-coaches-ask-listen-and-empathize
18. Collins, Jim. Good to Great. Williams Collins Publishers. 2001
19. Carey, Teresa. PBS News Hour. July 17, 2001. https://www.pbs.org/newshour/science/why-are-yawns-contagious-we-asked-a-scientist
20. Young, Matt, Soh, Nelson, Peake Stan. Life Literacy: Real Life Knowledge and Resources for the Next Generation to Succeed. Morgan James Publishers. 2021

21. https://www.businessballs.com/communication-skills/mehrabians-communication-theory-verbal-non-verbal-body-language/
22. Mattone, John. *The Intelligent Leader*. Wiley. 2020
23. Scudder, Tim. *Working With SDI 2.0.* Core Strengths Inc. 2021
24. Gladwell, Malcolm. *Outliers.* Back Bay Books. 2008
25. Blanchard, Ken. *The Heart of a Leader.* Honor Books. 1999
26. BrainFacts.org - https://www.brainfacts.org/in-the-lab/meet-the-researcher/2018/how-many-neurons-are-in-the-brain-120418
27. Newsweek.com July 15, 2020 https://www.newsweek.com/humans-6000-thoughts-every-day-1517963
28. Goldsmith, Marshall and Reiter, Mark. *The Earned Life.* Currency. 2022
29. Goggins, David. *Can't Hurt Me.* Lioncrest Publishing. 2018
30. Grover, Tim S. *Winning.* Scribner books. 2021
31. Kizer, Kristin. 36 POWERFUL LEADERSHIP STATISTICS [2022]: THINGS ALL ASPIRING LEADERS SHOULD KNOW. Jan 6, 2022. www.zippia.com
32. Arruda, William. 7 Soft Skills You Should Master To Advance Your Career. www.Forbes.com May 2, 2023 (https://www.forbes.com/sites/williamarruda/2023/05/02/7-soft-skills-you-should-master-to-advance-your-career/?sh=5c8ed1a73bc0)
33. https://www.garybertwistle.com/bio.html
34. https://en.wikipedia.org/wiki/Simone_Campbell
35. https://networklobby.org/about/srsimonebio/

36. NCADV Press kit: https://assets.speakcdn.com/assets/2497/ncadv_press_kit_.pdf
37. https://www.discovertheedge.com/nicole-jansen/
38. https://www.barrons.com/articles/20-minutes-with-clase-azul-tequila-founder-arturo-lomeli-01658763890
39. https://money.cnn.com/2017/07/04/smallbusiness/tequila-clase-azul-expensive/index.html
40. https://sonnymelendrez.com/san-antonio-motivational-speaker-biography/
41. https://ohiostatebuckeyes.com/staff/gene-smith/
42. https://www.bizjournals.com/columbus/news/2016/12/19/attendance-at-buckeyes-football-games-second-best.html
43. http://www.businessinsider.com/college-football-players-coaches-recruiting-2016-11
44. https://www.royalroads.ca/people/marilyn-taylor

About the Author

Stan Peake has spent the last 25 years helping thousands of leaders discover and live up to their potential. With entrepreneurial experience spanning eight businesses, Stan has started, bought into, closed, and sold businesses. As an executive, Stan has been a part of seven leadership teams in the last quarter century. He has hired, developed, and helped shape the careers of over 400 professionals in his career.

Stan holds a graduate certificate in values-based leadership from Royal Roads University, an executive education in Sales Leadership from Queens University, and a certificate in Entrepreneurship and Innovation from Harvard Business School. Stan is certified as an executive coach, a corporate facilitator, and as a practitioner of cultural transformation tools.

In his role as Co-Founder and Director of Leadership Development, Stan oversees the coaching and leadership development services for FSQ Consulting Inc, including a team of over 40 executive coaches in five countries. In 2023 FSQ Consulting was an Inc Magazine's Power Partner Award Winner, recognizing the best in B2B companies focused on helping other companies grow.

When not coaching others or leading FSQ's team of expert coaches, Stan is a regular speaker at business and leadership conferences. He has also written for several magazines and publications, including Entrepreneur, Bizztor Media (India's largest publication for entrepreneurs), and Choice Magazine, the industry magazine for coaches. US Insider listed Stan as one of the top 10 executive coaches to follow in 2023, alongside Tony Robbins and Jay Abraham. Stan's 2021 TEDx talk, "Lasting Happiness is an Inside Job" has been viewed over 114,000 times on YouTube.

Fixing Leadership is Stan's 9th book, six of his previous titles became bestsellers on Amazon, including the #1 bestsellers *How to Sell in Any Economy* and *Now What? 50 ways to build your business in a crisis*. Stan is also a business advisor and investor with a diverse portfolio of entrepreneurs and businesses he has been supporting since 2016.

Giving back is also very important to Stan and his family. Stan volunteers his time to speak at universities each year about leadership and entrepreneurship. Stan also organizes a neighborhood cleanup each Earth Day, 2024 being the 7th annual event. Peake is a regular contributor to the National Coalition Against Domestic Violence, as well as Operation Underground Railroad, which frees children from modern day slavery. Stan is on a mission to raise, donate, and organize donations of over $10 million dollars for worthy causes in his lifetime. Stan has also served on several volunteer boards, from children's organizations to local community organizations.

Stan resides in Calgary, AB, Canada with his wife Maria, son Chase, and dog Zeke.

To reach Stan:

Stan@getsuccessfaster.com • www.getsuccessfaster.com

www.ingramcontent.com/pod-product-compliance
Lightning Source LLC
Chambersburg PA
CBHW052159220526
45471CB00004B/1737